THE NINJA DEFENSE

Stephen K. Hayes

THE NINJA DEFENSE

A MODERN MASTER'S APPROACH TO UNIVERSAL DANGERS

TUTTLE Publishing

Tokyo | Rutland, Vermont | Singapore

Please note that the publisher and author of this instructional book are NOT RESPON-SIBLE in any manner whatsoever for any injury that may result from practicing the techniques and/or following the instructions given within. Martial arts training can be dangerous—both to you and to others—if not practiced safely. If you're in doubt as to how to proceed or whether your practice is safe, consult with a trained martial arts teacher before beginning. Since the physical activities described herein may be too strenuous in nature for some readers, it is also essential that a physician be consulted prior to training.

Published by Tuttle Publishing, an imprint of Periplus Editions (HK) Ltd.

www.tuttlepublishing.com

Copyright © 2012 Stephen K. Hayes
Technique action photographs by PRFranK.com

Library of Congress Cataloging-in-Publication Data
Hayes, Stephen K.
  The ninja defense : a modern master's approach to universal dangers / Stephen K. Hayes.
    p. cm.
  ISBN 978-4-8053-1211-7 (pbk.)
  1. Ninjutsu. I. Title.
  GV1114.73.H39 2012
  796.815--dc23
                          2012017562

ISBN 978-4-8053-1211-7

Distributed by

North America, Latin America & Europe
Tuttle Publishing
364 Innovation Drive, North Clarendon, VT 05759-9436 U.S.A.
Tel: 1 (802) 773-8930; Fax: 1 (802) 773-6993
Email: info@tuttlepublishing.com   Web: www.tuttlepublishing.com

Japan
Tuttle Publishing
Yaekari Building, 3rd Floor, 5-4-12 Osaki, Shinagawa-ku, Tokyo 141 0032
Tel: (81) 3 5437-0171; Fax: (81) 3 5437-0755
Email: sales@tuttle.co.jp   Web: www.tuttle.co.jp

Asia Pacific
Berkeley Books Pte. Ltd.
61 Tai Seng Avenue #02-12, Singapore 534167
Tel: (65) 6280-1330; Fax: (65) 6280-6290
Email: inquiries@periplus.com.sg   Web: www.periplus.com

First edition
16 15 14 13 12   10 9 8 7 6 5 4 3 2 1   1208CP

Printed in Singapore

TUTTLE PUBLISHING® is a registered trademark of Tuttle Publishing, a division of Periplus Editions (HK) Ltd.

Contents

Author Stephen K. Hayes, with hair grown long for his role in the NBC mini-series *Shogun*, and his teacher Masaaki Hatsumi during training in Japan in 1979.

Author's Introduction
WHO I AM AND WHY YOU CAN BELIEVE IN THIS PROGRAM

My first memory of seeing martial arts was an early 1950s *Lassie* TV show. In total amazement, I watched a small Japanese boy use his martial arts training to defeat a gang of American schoolyard bullies, and then later restore the health of his tormentors. You can learn such power of making there be rightness, having the capacity for harming if forced, healing if permitted? My young spirit was electrified. I had to have that!

After years of longing, I finally began my martial arts training as a teen in the 1960s at Miami University, in Oxford, Ohio, studying with returning Vietnam War combat vets. I had thought I would be learning the grappling method of judo, but it turned out to be a form of karate striking and kicking. I took to the training with near religious commitment, and my martial arts training became a primary part of my personal identity. There is a science of combat that empowers a gentle-of-spirit person to defeat a rough and brutal antagonist when necessary? I had to have that!

Monk warriors on the *Kung-Fu* TV show inspired me in the early 1970s. They possessed enlightened spiritual intelligence coupled with compassionate care for others on one hand, and awesome physical protector powers on the other. There really is a tradition of mythic greatness based on timeless ideals of self-development and fullness of awakening human potential? Realms of mind and even spiritual power in the martial arts? I had to have that!

James Bond book and movie references to ninja as invisible warriors inspired me to search for new heights of training beyond physical toughness. I moved to Japan in the mid-1970s and was accepted for training in the home dojo of Togakure Ryu ninja grandmaster Masaaki Hatsumi. All those martial art cliches about the power of mind being key to overcoming adversaries were really true, and facing hidden weaknesses in the depth of one's own soul was the first step to learning how to find and exploit an enemy's secret fears to paralyze him in combat? I had to have that!

Appalled that so few people would ever have access to what I had received through my ninja training in my teacher's secret dojo with his fifteen students in Japan, I vowed to share the timeless knowledge with the world. I vowed to make my teacher internationally recognized and a warrior icon in the eyes of his students. I promised to make him financially wealthy as well, to repay him for what he gave me, even when others urged him to cut me off as a cultural and racial outsider. I had to do that!

I taught public seminars in the 1980s as a way to test my skills and knowledge. From what I learned through trial by fire, I transformed into actual combat-useful tools the stylized *kihon* classical fundamentals I studied in Japan. Somehow, in the midst of challenge, the ancient lineage spoke to me and guided me on to discover the power and principles deep in the secret heart of the forms.

During years of travel and teaching, I met many wonderful people. Famous martial arts icons saw my passion and offered guidance from their paths. Magazine editors and television producers invited me to featured positions in articles and programs showcasing my work. Thousands of people around the world joined my once solitary practice of the ninja combat methods, and many of those students in turn became masterful practitioners themselves.

I also learned much about the depraved and cowardly side of human nature in those years. I was challenged by the envious and betrayed by a few who resented the idealism, risk, and hard work that led to my success. No exaggeration—by the mid-1980s, government agents were investigating actual murder plots against me.

I retired from public attention in the late 1980s in a form of retreat, roaming the world in search of spiritual adventure. Through seemingly impossible coincidences, I ended up traveling regularly with His Holiness the Dalai Lama as a protective escort throughout the 1990s. I was moved and inspired by his authentic heroic presence, a kingly greatness I had sought since childhood. Encouraged by my first-hand experience of the

Author Stephen K. Hayes served as personal security escort during Nobel Peace Prize Laureate His Holiness the Dali Lama's American visits in the 1990s.

Dalai Lama's spiritual intelligence and compassionate care for all, I vowed to offer the highest ideals of the warrior path to other seekers like me.

I founded a network of instructors in the 1990s for those who shared my passion for reaching the highest of human fulfillment by means of transforming the lowest of human instincts. Through realistic and honest training in how to defend against those degenerate enough to want to hurt others in order to feel pleasure, we can learn the principles for activating and unleashing the highest of our inherent human possibilities.

To provide western people the most useful and valuable personal protection training based on my study and testing of the historical Japanese ninja combat method, I had to do a lot of adapting. As a researcher, I enjoyed putting the historical puzzle pieces together to produce a useful defense method. At the same time, I knew very few people would be able or willing to spend years translating Japanese classics into modern western tools. In order to be of relevance in my home community, I had to adapt the ancient principles into a new and culturally relevant shape.

Fights in 1500s Japan were different from fights in 21st century America. Culture, laws, environmental factors—and even clothing of the time—influenced the development of Japan's feudal age fighting systems. Some major differences from today are important:

✦ Warriors in old Japan wore *kimono* robes with broad sleeves, *waraji* rice straw sandals tied to the bottoms of their feet, and various forms of *hakama* voluminous leggings.

✦ Genetically, the Japanese body trunk was long and the limbs short, when compared with Western people of today.

✦ Ground beneath the feet of battlers was either earth, grass, or in a few cases *tatami* rice straw matting.

✦ With no policing authority on patrol everywhere, law was often left in the hands of rival combatants, and so many a fight concluded with the ending of life to prevent the defeated from rising up to return for vengeance.

✦ In a state of unceasing warfare, people were psychologically conditioned to watch for the worst from any stranger approaching from a distance.

All these factors influenced the development of the ninja and samurai martial art of *taijutsu* 体術, literally translated as "the art or science of using the body in combat." In this classic Japanese fighting form, fighters strategically stayed far apart until the moment of clash, flexed their knees deeply to lower the seat close to the slippery or dusty ground, and often began attacks with long lunging footwork characteristic of Japanese sword cutting, where a right leg would step and propel a same-side right hand shove, grab, or stab.

Contrarily, in modern physical altercations, different factors come into play:

✦ People today wear form-fitting clothes with pockets that can conceal weapons, and hard-edged leather or rubber sole shoes.

✦ Genetically, the Euro-African ancestry body trunk is relatively short and the limbs long, when compared with people of ancient Japan.

✦ The ground is routinely hard, covered with concrete, blacktop, or wooden flooring, and is not so likely to be soft and giving.

✦ With strong police authority in the community, the law is very specific in limiting how far a citizen may go even in rightful self-defense against a criminal; sometimes the defender ends up in court facing judicial action against him for "too harsh" a defense.

✦ In an age of supposed enforced civility, people expect to be treated decently and to avoid wanton violence, giving a criminal a psychological advantage.

In contemporary fighting, an aggressor often uses extremely offensive language to intimidate or shock and then moves inside his intended victim's safety range before throwing hits or grabs. Fighters tend to hold their shoulders higher in variations of sport boxer postures with speed hand forward and power hand in back, and they move on quickly shuffling feet. Hands dart or swing in with rapid flurries of punches, slaps, grabs, and stabs rather than singular focused blows.

Bearing in mind so many differences in ancient Japanese and modern Western fight challenges, it seems obvious we need an updated method of ninja protector combat for today. It would not be the best route to rely on the details of an antique Japanese training system to solve modern American or European problems. On the other hand, the principles that made the Japanese fighting arts so effective are still valid, and I vowed to refurbished them to serve our new age.

It would be presumptuous of me to use an established historical name like *ninjutsu* to describe what I am offering as contemporary personal protection. For that reason I needed a term to differentiate between the classical ninja martial arts I was licensed by the grandmaster to teach and the modern adaptations I had developed. To label my modern derivation of the ancient *ninjutsu* principles, I created the new name To-Shin Do.

Even though new, the name is based on the structure of the old name. I separated the single letter character for *nin* 忍 of *ninja* and their secret art of *ninjutsu* into its two composite parts (with one small tweak). *To* 刀 for "sword" implies the technology we study. *Shin* 心 for "heart" reflects the cultivation of intelligence and intention. *Do* 道 translates as "road" or pathway to mastery.

It is important to remember that this is not something I just made up or pulled together from speculation. The martial art of To-Shin Do was born of the historical legacy behind three important roots of the ancient cultural heritage of Japan:

TO - Sword

From the *ninja* combat methods of the legendary phantom warriors born of Mt. Togakure and cultivated in the wooded mountains and marshes of Iga comes the core of our physical protection principles and strategies. To-Shin Do martial arts practice is a great way to reduce stress and increase strength, endurance, and flexibility, while fostering a sense of peace, security, and control in life.

SHIN - Spirit of intention

From the *kuji-kiri* intention-channeling training of the *shugenja* mountain spirit seekers of Mt. Yoshino comes the essence of our program for the discovery and development of the key qualities that characterize a fully actualized human being. We can achieve a more focused and disciplined understanding of the cause and effect dynamics that lead to success and fulfillment in life.

DO - Path to mastery

From the originally Himalayan esoteric *vajrayana mikkyo* mind and spirit sciences of Mt. Hiei comes the technique of cultivating into powers our mental, emotional, and spiritual potentials. We can learn skillful ways to transform the inner and outer challenges of life into success, and ultimately come to grips with the question of how to experience directly the significance of life itself.

From deep roots in the principles of classic Japanese ninja martial arts, To-Shin Do training is a thorough system of personal preparation for facing the kinds of conflict and opposition that can surprise us in the course of daily living. Our training program leads to the ability to live life fully, fearlessly, and freely.

The lessons in our training method are based on ancient well-tested warrior disciplines handed down through historical martial traditions I studied with the ninja grandmaster in Japan, along with the spiritual and ethical lessons I learned traveling with the Dalai Lama of Tibet. At the same time, To-Shin Do training is built around a very modern approach to handling successfully the kind of threats and confrontations most likely in our own contemporary culture, and for seeking answers to to the deepest questions of life.

To-Shin Do is a realistic martial arts training system that includes instruction in techniques and strategies for dealing with:

✦ grappling, throwing, choking, and joint-locking
✦ striking, kicking, and punching
✦ stick, blade, cord, and projectile weapons
✦ handling multiple assailants and surprise attacks
✦ overcoming psychological intimidation or bullying

Beyond the basic training that leads to Black Belt in To-Shin Do is a collection of optional advanced courses including:

✦ first-response emergency medical treatment
✦ methods for survival in hostile environments
✦ security protection for dignitaries

+ law enforcement specialties
+ intelligence gathering systems
+ how to instruct classes and run a school
+ classical Japanese weapons.

Through exposure to the physical, intellectual, and spiritual challenges posed in the many facets of our training program, you will gain first-hand experience in identifying and enhancing those aspects of your life that facilitate growth, confidence, peace of mind, and the joy that accompanies living well and powerfully. To-Shin Do martial arts self development promotes a *mandala* of 5 spheres of life-fulfilling aspects each of us desires to experience:

1. **Abundance** – Authority to cast your own definition of success – living a rich and important life, seeing the value of all you encounter.
2. **Authenticity** – Knowledge of your own true nature – realizing personal peace through intelligence, seeing things as they truly are.
3. **Association** – Connection to friends, family, and allies – expressing who you really are and sharing respect and admiration with others.
4. **Accomplishment** – A sense that you are needed – fighting the good fight to serve a worthy cause way bigger than you as an individual.
5. **Actualization** – Personal fulfillment – time and space to live up to your dreams and see the big picture of how significant life is.

To-Shin Do martial arts training is founded on a very strong and bluntly stated code of mindful action—how to live a worthy noble life. You cannot learn how to become a winner by spending time with losers. Ally yourself with proven role models who have been through the battles and can demonstrate what powerful living looks like, and you develop the momentum of accomplishment that leads to being a winner in life.

I am still inspired to this day by those exaggerated images of intelligence, compassion, and strength I saw in those novels, TV shows, and movies of my youth. There is a tradition of inspiration for people longing for the taste of mythic-level self-expansion in pursuit of an ideal so high that we never will surpass it? I have to have that!

Preparation for the cultivation of new strengths begins with intelligence gathering. Enjoy this book, and any new awareness it sparks in your life. Share its ideas with others. Remember to re-read these chapters several times. Look for the direct applications to life right now, and use the insights to plan ahead for future confidence and power. By all means, use it to inspire ever more happiness in your life. The world needs your bright strength.

A To-Shin Do belt rank promotion is an invitation to enter
the next phase of personal challenge.

Chapter One

HONEST AND RELIABLE PREPARATION FOR REAL THREATS

I still remember the first time I was threatened with stupid pointless violence. I was in kindergarten, walking down a school hallway in line with classmates in 1954. The boy walking next to me, a complete stranger, turned to me and said, "I bet I can lick you."

I was perplexed by the boy's odd comment. "Lick me"? His words made no sense, but I nonetheless felt an ominous ugliness. At home I was used to affection, intelligence, and courtesy, so I could not immediately identify the violence implied by his words. Still, I sensed that something creepy was going on. I had never been assaulted by anyone, but down in my bones I somehow knew the boy did not have friendship in mind.

I was five years old and knew nothing of territorial imperative or a need to assert my manly image. I did not know how or why to act tough. In confused innocence I replied, "Yeah. I bet."

The boy seemed content with that and we walked on wordlessly. It was over. He had won something he wanted. I was not harmed at all, but something inside me had changed. I had sensed my vulnerability at the hands of another who lived by values far different from mine. The boy had not even touched me, but I felt violated. The icy casualness of his desire to humiliate another child left me unsettled and sent me on a life-time search for a dignified foundation of personal security.

Healthy people want to live life in a happy, expressive, and positive manner. Therefore, healthy people usually prefer to avoid situations and individuals that would impede the freedom to live a satisfying, stimulating, and meaningful life. For healthy people, the idea of enjoying willfully fighting with others seems odd or perverse or even sad.

Not seeking out fights in life, and thereby having little reference for handling confrontation, can leave us awkwardly unprepared for random violence when it does happen, though. For many people in these days of fragmented communities, transient workplaces, and overcrowded prisons, fear of falling victim to violent crime is a common impediment to the freedom to be happy. Think about it. Do you know anyone who might choose to limit life and avoid certain places or certain activities because of concern for danger?

Conflicts to be avoided are not just physical assaults. There are many ways to be defeated. For some in these days of fierce economic pressures generated by an ever changing international marketplace, danger appears in veiled forms that threaten to undercut the personal financial security needed to sustain a family. For others in these days of disintegrating cultural values and their emerging hollow and disjointed replacements, threats to personal fulfillment take even more subtle guises to sap the energy and defeat the will to prevail.

If we are not careful, without realizing what we are doing, we can end up assisting our adversaries to succeed in their attacks against us. We get in our own way because we do not understand the thinking process in the mind of the kind of person who enjoys violent treatment of others. To add to the difficulty, we do not have a clear picture of how we ourselves operate when under the pressure of threats, whether those threats be physical, economical, or emotional. Indeed, most of the children I went to school with in the 1950s were encouraged to defuse and smooth over confrontation. We were taught to consider threats as misunderstandings. Our mothers admonished us that mean people would go away if we just ignored them long enough. Few of us were taught how to stare danger in the eye and make it fear us.

This volume is an intelligent approach towards learning how to survive encounters with dangerous people, including situations requiring rescue of others from danger. We start with solutions for the most likely and most common forms of assault and build from there. I call it intelligent because it includes a lot of knowledge routinely absent from more primitive systems of self-defense training in how to fight.

Based on over 40 years of observation, I believe that most martial arts books and schools completely overlook the crucial area of training the mind and spirit as an effective part of the overall self-protection unit. Of course many martial arts programs *imply* that you will be sharper, more resourceful, cooler under fire, more disciplined and more determined to win as a result of their training, but there is little actual instruction in how to accomplish such personal elevation. In crude programs like that, you are expected to just keep banging away at training and the advanced life skill capabilities you hope for will somehow magically emerge and mature despite lack of direct instruction in such qualities.

What if there were a reliably effective way to prepare yourself for conflict and confrontation in potentially dangerous streets, unpredictably troubled workplaces, and too-often unstable family homes while still maintaining a hopeful or optimistic outlook on life? What if there were a way to stay prepared for a violent clash without sinking into a pained mind-set of isolation and cold aloofness towards others? What if there were a way to build your awareness of personal security without losing the freedom to be trusting and joyous? What if there were a program that could show you how to feel more confident while not requiring you to dedicate your life to unabated alienating toughness? What if there were a way to prepare for possible conflict without having to become as cruel or brutish as the loathsome characters who take pleasure in violent damage to others?

My program emphasizes an ethic of learning to be a *protector as opposed to a predator.* Sure, some schools give lip service to such ideals, but evidence shows there is still a lot of loud aggressive ego even among some highly rated martial artists. I am disappointed to say that I have met too many martial arts teachers still controlled by the inner demon fears of inadequacy and insecurity that led them to seek instruction in how to fight in the first place. Sadly, beneath any noble creed can still lurk a need to present oneself as the roughest, meanest, or cruelest. Check and see. Flip through any popular martial arts magazine and count the photos of those who cultivate the look of tough criminals or thugs—the very monsters we train to protect against!

Our ideal is to become a *tatsujin*—a fully actualized person of accomplishment. The point of our training is creating *more strength and safety in the world*, instead of seeking thrill through hurting, beating, or conquering others.

If your martial arts training does not cause you to grow as a human being, such training can actually add to your pain in life. Without evolving and becoming stronger and bigger internally, you are stranded in a place where you have highly cultivated skills for hurting other people and yet are still dominated by internalized angers and fears collected in younger days of vulnerability. Do you really want to study how to be strong from a person whose fierce bristly external armor is but a brittle shell holding back the leftover childhood rage and loneliness he hopes you will never see in him?

This book is written for real people seeking realistic answers to real problem possibilities. Over the years, I've interviewed law enforcement officers, security professionals, emergency room doctors—and even coroners—to find the twelve most common attacks likely to be thrown at good people by dangerous aggressors. I then adapted the technique principles I learned from my decades of ninja *taijutsu* martial arts study and developed a first line of training to show people how to defend against these assaults. Begin your adventure with a look at how to win in the twelve assault types most likely to occur in a dangerous confrontation, how to work in those twelve threat situations to rescue yourself or other people, how to use twelve natural body self-defense tools, and how to develop the grounded presence of focused command in high-pressure situations.

I am first to acknowledge the training scenarios in this book are not the breathtaking exotic stuff of martial arts fantasy movies. I also do not hide the fact that seven of the twelve attacks covered in this book would be unlikely to show up in a prize fight arena, ring, or cage. The material here is neither for entertainment nor contest. These skills and insights are what you would want your loved ones to know if they ever had to walk some mean streets or make their way home from realms of predators. Less cool. More tool.

I admit my ego had to struggle with choosing a reality premise for this book. It is so tempting to just show off. I do have plenty of amazing tricky techniques I teach at my martial arts school, and a few friends urged me to make this an edgy and over-the-top book to impress others and celebrate my own decades of training for mastery.

I nonetheless chose to go with the ground of reality for this volume. A few of my other books teach some of my martial art's more advanced skills, and my purpose in writing this book now after a lifetime of practice is not to show off or impress other martial arts masters. I have been asked by many people to present the *distilled truth* of what makes up the most important lessons in how to protect the good and the pure from the cruel and brutal. This then is indeed that. Here is the curriculum I wish I could have studied in my early days of passion for the martial arts when I began my training odyssey back in the 1960s.

The self-training program in this book and DVD gives you a solid and reliable foundation for learning how to prevail over violent aggressors. There are three sections to each lesson.

First, you will study a fundamental response for each problem. *What do you do when you suddenly must intervene to protect yourself or someone else?* These fighting hits and grabs are called "the basics" in English, or *kihon* in the original Japanese language, and are your primary fighting tools.

Next, you will study a defense against each of these rescues gone bad. *What if a confused or violent person uses the same skills to attack you or another?* Practice each *kata*, or "fight scenario form," over and over as a way to learn to recognize the problem, condition yourself to find the right answer for the problem every time, and internalize *how it feels to win*.

Finally, you will practice your skills full-power and full-speed against training targets to advance your fighting attributes. *How powerfully, quickly, and precisely can you move?* You need to build muscle strength and flexibility, improve effective balance when you move quickly, and develop more fitness, finesse, and focus.

Depending on your level of expertise, you can practice each *kata* defensive action sequence with training partners approaching from appropriately progressing degrees of challenge:

"I'm new at this" - Practice the defense from a set place against a stationary simulated aggressor with a designated right or left attack

"I'm learning this" - Practice the defense from a set place against a stationary simulated aggressor who sends an attack from right or left without predesignation

"I'm getting this" - Practice the defense from a set place against a moving simulated aggressor who continuously changes position around you and then sends an attack at you from right or left

"I'm good" - Practice the defense while you move and change position against a likewise moving simulated aggressor who sends an attack from right or left

"I'm really good" - Practice the defense while on the move against a moving simulated aggressor who moves against you from right or left, and in multiple movement flow combinations with additional techniques from the same block of three lessons in the chapter

"I've got this down" - Practice the defense while on the move against one or more moving simulated aggressors who attack from right or left, as part of a multiple strike flow combination with additional strike or grab attacks from the entire series of twelve lessons.

This program delivers the twin benefits of efficient training for overcoming dangerous people and situations along with effective foundation building for personal self-development and well-being. If you are less vulnerable to humiliation or damage, you are more likely to be at ease in more situations with more people. The more at ease you are in more situations, the more likely you are to experience more peace in life. The more inner peace you find as a result of increased outer security, the more likely you are to cultivate enhanced health and happiness from less stress and tension. The healthier and happier you appear to be, the more other healthy and happy people will want to be around you. You win.

Author Stephan K Hayes' wife Rumiko demonstrates a classical bojutsu long staff defense against the Japanese sword from the historical ninja martial arts at root of To-Shin Do as modern self-protection training.

Chapter Two

MAKING THE CHOICE TO FIGHT

Ever found yourself in a situation where others had gained the upper hand dealing with you? You were strategically at a disadvantage. They may have been physically superior; they were bigger, better trained, or holding deadlier weapons. Their tactics may have been superior; they had a plan to confuse you or hook your emotions. They may have held a psychological advantage; they commanded fear based on reputation or a fierce and crazy spirit ready for conflict, or they hid behind some disguise of weakness to get you to drop your guard.

You felt trapped. Initially, you did not recognize the need to take command of the situation, and then it was too late to get away. With escape now impossible, you were forced into action with only two choices. One possibility was to give in and let them take what they wanted. Such a choice is called submitting. The other possibility was to move to stop them from succeeding in their assault. That choice is called fighting.

Why fight when winning is not important?

Fighting is not the only way to respond to attackers, of course. You do not have to beat everyone who wants to fight. Some confrontations have no compelling power over you, and submitting has no cost because you perceive no threat of loss. A guy rants insultingly about a team you do not know in a sport you do not follow. So what? A driver cuts you off for the last parking space near the mall entrance as you drive around to the rear package pickup door. So what? An office sneak plots to cheat you out of your job as you finalize plans for early retirement in a new dream home. So what?

Why fight in such cases where animosity directed against you has no effect on the quality of your day? There is no point in resisting hostility just for the sake of resisting. There is no need to bark back at barking dogs. Compulsive competitive retaliation for the sole purpose of defeating someone else regardless of the prize is a pathetic form of neurotic behavior.

There are as well non-resisting ways to avoid the harm of directly hostile people. Walk away from the loudmouths. Let the guy butt into line. Ignore the one pumping his obscene hand gesture at you in traffic. You are morally bigger than they are. Your life is better than theirs. You can graciously give a break to an occasional low-life clod.

Though non-resistance can be a viable way to handle aggression from others, you will eventually reach a limit as to how far you can go without having to take a stand on something. It is also true that non-resistance to hostility against you will have a price, even if it is only a subtle psychic cost. When antagonism would indeed affect your life, something of importance must always be given up for non-resistance to do the job of returning life to a peaceful condition.

What about those situations where you can not afford to give away what is demanded? What about times you do not dare give another control over your resources? What about when you cannot tolerate a bully victimizing your child? What about when you cannot let your body be savaged by an abuser?

A fight is actively resisting hostile actions directed against you.

There are times when non-resistance is neither possible nor acceptable. You may be compelled to stop an unbearable assault. Passive responses must be ruled out in a reasonable discussion of coping with truly *intolerable* aggression. The intolerable nature of such abuse will prompt a natural desire to fight the destructive consequences of your assailant's intentions. You know you will not survive if this person gains control over you. Life will be lessened irreparably. You have to resist. You have to fight. You have to take direct action to counter the damaging potential of the hostility aimed at you.

How do you learn to handle assaults in those times when reasoning, running, hiding, or giving in are not acceptable responses to the threat? How do you develop the capacity to stand firm when the price of non-resistance is too dear to pay for peace? You need to practice how to go into action effectively when you are forced into conflict by everything that constitutes your values, your ideals, your sense of responsibility, your duty, and your very survival.

Prepare for attacks in different forms from different approaches

Body Attack – Obviously, you can be attacked physically. One or more people or animals can come at you with the intention to impair, harm, or kill you. A physical attack and its resultant resistance is probably what most of us call "fighting" in the popular sense of the word.

Mind Attack – You can be attacked mentally. Through spoken or written or even implied words, people can attack you with intention to impede or diminish you, or drive you into some form of submission. A mental attack and its resultant verbalized resistance is what we call "arguing."

Spirit Attack – You can be attacked on the essential or spiritual level. By means of deception, disguised subtle aggression, and unstated or denied challenges, people can come at you with the intention to reduce or eliminate your influence, take control of your options, or cause you to work unknowingly for their best interests against your own. A spirit attack and its resultant inner turmoil is what we call "psychological warfare," or a "battle of wits."

A truly determined antagonist knows that any of the three body-mind-spirit factors can be combined to make it even more difficult for you to respond directly and effectively. Experienced aggressors attack with startling suddenness from the foggy edges of your distracted perception or diverted preparation. Deception has always been a primary tool of invaders throughout the ages.

✦ Constant harping arguments over minor things could be a ruse to wear down your will; the point or topic of the argument does not matter at all if the final effect is you giving up your stand.

✦ Frustrating hassles that drain the strength of your intention could be a set-up for physical attack; you are more accessible as a target if you are distracted from sensing the assault coming.

✦ Physical abuse—anything from overloading you at work to actual blows to your body—could be a way to defeat the power of your mind; it is hard for superior philosophy to triumph when you are desperately struggling for physical survival.

The most dangerous adversaries will come at you from all three angles at once. The most cunning aggressor will put you in position to be *physically overwhelmed* while *mentally confused* while questioning at your core just what is *your rightful role* as the situation sweeps you along.

If you know how to recognize the tactics of experienced aggressors, you can scientifically avoid being drawn into their areas of power over you. You can then strategically move the conflict into your own area of power and security, and watch them retreat or go down:

✦ You can force a physically superior attacker to operate on the level of mental strategy

✦ You can force a devious workplace conniver to compete in the realm of verifiable physical results

✦ You can force the will-sapping "energy vampire" to struggle with you cheerfully ignoring their covert aggression.

The most sensible counsel or shrewdest advice is to avoid going face to face and toe to toe with skillful adversaries in their own realms of power. Do not get tricked into trading punches with a professional fighter. Do not get conned into chess matches with chess champions. Do not get fooled into popularity contests with people who have no principles when it comes to seducing the masses. Get the chess champ into the boxing ring. Trick the cage fighter into a TV debate. Force the office schemer into a sales contest to determine who wins the promotion.

It is important to acknowledge that if you are not in a refereed contest of fighting skills or a structured play of martial techniques as art performance, there are no consensual rules to protect you. Conversely, in street self protection situations, though there are no rules to limit you, there are laws that govern applicability of your self-defense actions. You are compelled to draw on everything you can summon to put you in the position of advantage. Make the adversaries have to change and adapt to your dictates. Make it hard for them to make it hard on you. You do not have to fight them on their terms.

Chapter Three

FOUNDATIONAL UNDERSTANDING FOR WINNING

I t is important to acknowledge the specific differences between self-defense, fighting skills, and martial arts. Some people fail to understand or recognize this important distinction, though. Techniques, tactics, mental states, emotional considerations, laws, and cultural conditions make self-defense on the street a very different challenge when compared to willful fighting in a contest or imitating stylized combat from a foreign culture of ages past. Do not assume a skilled martial artist or fighting contest winner would be adept in a self protection confrontation on the street. It would also be inappropriate to expect every self-defense expert to be an artist in motion. The three areas of training certainly can overlap, but they are not necessarily the same thing and training in one area does not guarantee expertise in another.

Self-defense

Personal protection self-defense training is preparation for winning in situations where you suddenly and unexpectedly find yourself under siege. You do not see the attack coming. Most likely you are not even thinking about fighting. Your surprise and lack of preparation are often part of a predator's deliberate strategy. In a self-defense scenario, as quickly as possible you need to recognize the attack, overcome it, and escape to safety. In some self-defense confrontations, shrewd psychological positioning and clever verbal response may be of even more importance than top notch fitness or champion level expertise.

Fighting skill

Hand-to-hand combat fighting skill is related to but different from self-defense. When challenged to a fight, you know an assault is coming, and you move into action with the intent of winning the fight. Perhaps escape is neither possible nor the best or most appropriate choice. Perhaps there are others who need your protection. Perhaps you need to restrain a criminal from doing more damage. Perhaps through fighting you send a message that will prevent worse violence in the future. Whatever the valid motivation, you choose to fight when challenged and you intentionally engage your attacker(s) with skill. You willfully stay in the fight with the goal of subduing the aggressor to bring the assault to a close on your terms.

Martial arts as a path in life

Related to self-defense skills (*you do not expect the attack...*) and combat skills (*you know you have to fight...*) is a realm of physical, mental, and spiritual training through which practicing techniques of combat is used to facilitate personal development. Through martial arts study you explore lessons grander and deeper than just fighting. Such lessons prepare you to win in all sorts of situations, even those not physical in their threat. In pursuing the path of the noble warrior through martial arts training, your life increasingly reflects the depth of the qualities you seek

Author Stephen K. Hayes became one of the most talked about martial arts teachers in the USA in the 1980s, and was inducted into the Black Belt Hall of Fame.

through your study. The highest goals of martial arts training are most often perfection of character, commitment to bettering the world, and attainment of personal peace.

So, how to build self-defense skill expertise?

Begin your training as a protector with a first step of developing your sense of personal accountability when it comes to security. It might be argued that attack encounters do not occur in a vacuum, and are not isolated and unrelated to anything else happening in the world. Anyone claiming total surprise at a hostile confrontation might with proper coaching recall subtle but nonetheless distinct hunches and warning signs from the environment that were overlooked, overridden, or brushed aside.

Predators have predictable ways of thinking and operating. Use a knowledge of how aggressors victimize others to prepare to defeat those who would prey upon you. Accept the reality of criminal threats in the world and make up your mind not to be a victim. The denial and passivity that many people retreat into when it comes to violent crime makes the predator's work even easier. Defeating an aggressor absolutely must start with knowledge that there are predators out there, and a firmly made promise not to be an easy target.

Human predators, just like their animal counterparts, hope to take what they want with little risk of getting hurt or killed. They survey the population and look for an easy target who is not paying attention and who looks like the type who will not put up much of a fight. They then set up the situation to maximize their advantages and minimize the target's chances of escape or counterattack.

Five key considerations

Awareness in five key areas can help you address the possibilities for effective personal safety in a world that can sometimes turn threatening. What are you doing proactively to increase the likelihood of returning home happy and healthy every day? What can you alter in your daily routine to increase your likelihood of safety? How can you reduce unnecessary exposure to bad people, bad places, and bad times?

This collection of five key awareness considerations does not really follow an ordered list as they appear here; there is no 1 through 5 ranking. Any of the five could be your first area of consideration and strength building. Each of the five areas of awareness finds its reflection in all of the other four.

External Awareness

Develop the habit of taking a natural healthy curious interest in your surroundings from moment to moment. What do you notice?

- ✦ What's going on?
- ✦ Where are you?
- ✦ Who is near you?
- ✦ Do you feel safe?
- ✦ What happens next?

Internal Awareness

Make a habit of self-reflection. How do you feel about yourself, in relation to what's going on?

- ✦ Self esteem – Are *you* worth defending?
- ✦ Strengths – What are your *options* in the situation?
- ✦ Susceptibility – What habits have gotten you in trouble before?
- ✦ Strategies – What's the *best way* to get what you need?

Body Language

Do you look like someone who is in charge of life, or like someone who is waiting for *somebody else* to take charge? Do you look like an easy target? What do you communicate about yourself to others by the way you:

- ✦ Talk?
- ✦ Walk?
- ✦ Dress?
- ✦ Carry yourself?

Boundaries

- ✦ At what point does offensive behavior and speech from others go from tolerable to unacceptable?
- ✦ Do others know where you "draw the line"?
- ✦ How do you communicate your boundaries?
- ✦ What do you do when someone does not listen or does not acknowledge your boundaries?

Preparation

Work in advance to be prepared to do what it takes to get home healthy and happy. How ready are you?

Work on stocking up experience and understanding. Build the power of knowledge that comes with, "Been there, won that!" Make a point of enjoying attentively studying, reading about, and exploring:

+ The news ("What's the latest as to *where* I don't want to be and *who* I don't want to see?")
+ The law ("What are my *options* if invaded?")
+ Human anatomy ("What targets produce the *most* results with the *least* risk and smallest expenditure of energy?")
+ Predator behavior (Are they huffing, puffing, and bluffing—or downright deadly?)
+ Human nature (Can I give them something to let them feel like they won, without losing something important to me?)

Work on physical conditioning for peak performance. Build strength, health, and presence. Carry yourself like a confident winner, and most often bullies will look elsewhere for their victim.

Work on physical training in effective techniques. Practice what works. Find the best teachers sharing authentic principles and realistic techniques in ways that build your understanding of how to prevail in challenging situations. Toughen up. Build your skills.

Work on building up honest confidence through conscientious practice. Like a ship weathering a storm in a fortified harbor, take refuge in your potential for developing strength, your effective path of preparation, and the wise counsel of those who have been there before you. Based on your training experience, develop:

+ Confident authentic belief in your potential (*"I can do this!"*)
+ Confident discipline for what you study (*"This stuff works!"*)
+ Confident respect for your teachers and training partners who share with you their secrets of success (*"These people bring out my best!"*)

Work on psychological conditioning through positive training. Pay attention to paying attention, and catch yourself when you slide into negative or self-doubt thinking. Watch out for the temptation to slip into distraction or denial when confronted by things you do not like to deal with or think about. Become strong by facing and building up your areas of weakness without apology and by celebrating and sharing with others all that makes up your areas of strength. Old habits die hard, so vow to be extra nurturing of your new ideals.

Chapter Four

RECOGNIZE HOW DANGER ESCALATES

As a student of a personal protection program based on fighting principles developed for intelligence gatherers in Japan centuries ago, you are training to promote more security in the world. With the goal of more safety on the streets and in the schools and at the workplace, it is helpful to explore and understand a rational hierarchy of progressing phases of escalating demand for defensive techniques.

The ninja knew that the best way to defeat predators is to be invisible in their eyes. If they do not know you exist, they cannot gain access to you. Next best is to convince the predator not to choose you as a victim. If you look well prepared, you look difficult to victimize. Not the best nor most preferred way to maintain security, but nonetheless a possible requirement to be sure the good person goes home happy and healthy, is to fight back way more effectively than a predator would have imagined you could.

In a martial art dedicated to shielding good people from the insanity and horror of predatory violent aggression, there are several possibilities for handling hostile encounters without having to resort to physically engaging another person in a fight. Bear in mind the objective is to stay as safe and happy as possible throughout your day, not to go hunting for all the rats and rascals in your community so you can "give 'em a good lesson." We are committed to creating and sustaining honest peace in the world. We are not seeking out and relishing opportunities to stir up more violence.

In a fighting contest, you know the intention of the person across from you. Out in the world, it may be more difficult to know what is ahead. An aggressor stepping in front of you may very well be a dangerous predator, experienced and practiced in the ways of shattering bright lives as a brawler, robber, rapist, or killer. Or those giving you a hard time may just be rough people who feel your presence in their space or on their turf is some kind of challenge. It is also just as possible that the person raging at you is a normally harmless citizen now temporarily confused and out of control over some unexpected frustration. What is your best defense? A kind word, a firm warning, a kick to the stomach, a gun barrel under the jaw? How will you know the best thing to do?

The following description of phases of progression in the need for defense may inspire you to train for as many protection options as possible. At the top of the list is simply not being where hostility roams. Fighting other people is way down on the list of best solutions to conflict or confrontation. By no means is an angry fistfight your top choice in every rude encounter. Your ideal is to bring about peace. Your hope is to do that before things degenerate to a brutal scuffle against a person who feels he has nothing to lose.

1. Plan ahead for safety

Make it hard for danger to pin you down. Start with developing the habit of proactively planning to avoid conditions that could lead to the need for self-defense.

Disappear from danger. Structure your life so that no one thinks of making you their target. You will need a set of plans to:

- ✦ Protect your home—when you and loved ones are there, and when nobody is there
- ✦ Protect you and your loved ones while away from home—at school, at work, while traveling, etc.
- ✦ Protect your assets not kept at home or in your pocket that are vulnerable to fraud and theft.

Be proactive. Make a commitment to living a fulfilling life as free as possible from stress-inducer dangers. Set your life up to encourage pleasant days. As much as you can, surround yourself with happy, healthy, positive, and productive people. Pick a place to live where you are least likely to run into violence. Choose a job where confrontation potential suits your temperament comfortably. Reject the powerlessness of thinking you have no choice when it comes to the people and places your life brings you.

Once you have positioned yourself to be as free as possible from potential violence and hostility, set up passive measures of protection. Create external safety structures and procedures for your home and workplace. Effective lighting, sturdy locks, clear lines of vision, secure parking, a reduced profile not flaunting wealth or privilege, and discrete name usage in public listings help make it difficult for violence to find you and gain access to you.

Next, set things up to be ready for emergency escape so you can disappear from danger if need be. Plan evacuation routes, concealment spots, and caches of defense tools like flashlight, whistle, and appropriate weapons at home and work. Keep your car ready for possible emergencies, tuned up and gassed up and equipped with route finders and basic medical and survival protection kits.

Ever-changing social and cultural realities require heightened alertness and tactical adaptability to counter sophisticated subtle threats. Some of the most damaging attacks you could face could be carried out remotely. How do we as martial arts students train to defend against cyber crime like identity theft? How do we defeat cyber bullying where lives are shattered by cruel personal attacks and slanders? Are protective measures against such not directly physical attacks valid subjects for self-defense study?

2. Actively scan for danger

Beyond skillful passive preparation, practice scanning for the possibility of danger. Pay attention when you are out and about away from areas where you normally control with confidence your degree of safety and security.

Keep your senses open for hints of trouble. Be on the lookout for suspicious behavior or conversations. Tune into the energy of your surroundings. Be ready to go some place better for you if you sense something is wrong. Certainly enjoy a cheerful attitude towards life, relish your daily opportunities for new adventures, but do not become fooled into disregarding the potential for bumping into harm.

Stay alert. Notice the numbers and positions and look of people around you in public places. Consciously assess any threatening individuals. Note their size and strength, their demeanor, apparent emotional state, and position in relation to you. What are the messages behind their movements, dress, and deportment? Look for possible escape routes if things should go bad. Identify things that could serve as barriers and shields against attack. Scan for possible objects you could pick up and use as defensive weapons if needed.

Stay conscious of your own state from moment to moment. What are your strengths? What are your weaknesses or limitations? What is your level of proficiency with self-defense skills? How do your feelings and mood in the moment impact what you are experiencing and seeing? Do any possible legal or social considerations influence your choices of action? What is the smartest move if danger comes near to you?

3. Evacuate to safety

When you feel endangered, just leave. Get out of there when things turn suspicious, creepy, or threatening.

Go someplace else where danger is less likely to reach you. Leaving for a safer spot will give you the best possibility for avoiding physical and emotional wear and tear and injury, not to mention avoiding follow-up legal repercussions that could interrupt your life as a result of a fight.

Even winning a fight can have its costs. You might pay a price for coming out on top; the loser could get in a good shot before going down, or you could damage your hand knocking him out. Your life could be disrupted and your time wasted; police will want to get involved, legal charges could be pressed against you. Follow-up difficulties could show up after you thought the fight was over; the defeated troublemaker could win a judgement against you, or commit to a vendetta of revenge against you.

When someone tries to initiate an inappropriate conversation or spark a conflict, you can just walk away without a word or a glance. Just leave. If you need to break an uncomfortable connection with someone you do not want to deal with, you can create a ruse to make it look like you did not notice the threatened aggression. Act like you just remembered something and turn abruptly and walk away. Pat a pocket or two like you are missing something and walk back to the safe place you came from. Reach in your pocket and pull out a phone as though you got an important call and walk off looking for quieter space.

Just leave. Do not get pulled into further conversation. Do not reply to an aggressor's accusations. Do not argue. Do not apologize or explain what you are doing. Do not dignify them by justifying yourself. Keeping the aggressor in your attention so you cannot be hit or grabbed from behind, walk away. Go where it is safe and sane and you are welcomed and appreciated.

4. Defuse the tenseness

Take charge of the confrontation and defuse the tenseness if there is still time or space to interact effectively. Perhaps you can use words and physical cues to change the tone of the moment and convince an agitated or belligerent person that rationality is a better route to resolution.

Remember to maintain a higher level of awareness than the other person. You will need a more secure sense of centeredness and broader vision than the person opposing you. Stay elevated. Be mindful to avoid being pulled down to lower level anger and loss of emotional control.

Project a calm presence by breathing deeply and regularly. Hold a confident and alert facial expression and body posture. Maintain eye contact with the person. Move with calming ease and avoid sudden or jerky actions that could surprise the agitated or dangerous person and spark their attack.

Carefully position yourself where you can defend if you cannot calm the aggressor and things blow up. Stay out of reach. Put a barrier between yourself and the antagonist if you can. Stand off-center and angle yourself so you can pull back from a sudden strike or grab. Keep your hands free, unencumbered or empty if possible, and ready for action.

Speak slowly and evenly. Keep your voice calm and low. Avoid threats, insults, demands, condescending statements, or any words that would give the other person further cause for blowing out of control. Acknowledge the agitated person's feelings if it might bring the situation to a calmer level. "I can see how you would feel angry..."

If necessary, you can say something to excuse yourself without opening up further challenge. "Hey, I'm just looking for someplace to get a beer and watch the ball game. I don't need to fight. I'm leaving." You can use gracious but nonetheless firm language. "I appreciate the invitation but I have friends I promised to visit. Thanks. I'm off."

With extreme care, you might use confident light humor to make yourself the butt of the joke. Being careful not to appear weak, show the other person you have no need to fight and defeat them. Say with a wry smile, "You're the third person today who wants to kick my tail. Man, I'm aggravating everybody today. Let me just get out of here and quit bothering you."

5. Confront and dissuade

Interrupt the aggressor's momentum towards violence and command him to leave you alone. Actively and directly resist the aggressor's demands and demonstrate your unwillingness to submit in the way such a person expects from a victim.

Some people will not allow you to de-escalate the violent build-up because they actually like confronting others and making them uncomfortable. Such aggressors enjoy intimidating and exerting power over others. They are driven by a need to control, dominate, and humiliate. Showdowns are their stock in trade.

An attack could begin with the aggressor testing you out. He may try a few words or actions to see whether you resist or submit, in effect interviewing you for the role of victim. Your confident assertive refusal to go along with such offense in the early stages of testing may give him cause to move on in search of a more submissive target.

Firmly stand your ground in a confident and watchful manner. Maintain eye contact. Avoid movements that could hint at timidity or lack of resolve. Breathe deeply and regularly and state in your deepest voice that you will not be controlled or intimidated. "Stop it now. Back away from me." State in direct language that you know what they are doing. "I don't like the threatening tone of your voice. Do not speak to me like that." Make reasonable firm commands for what you want done. "We have nothing to discuss. You get in your car and I'll get in my car and we'll both get on with our lives." Communicate your expectations clearly. "This conversation is over. I want you to move away from me right now."

Call attention to yourself with your voice and actions. Make it clear to all who might move to aid you that you are resisting offensive behavior. Let everyone know you will not tolerate abuse, you are not fooled by what is going on, you do not want any connection with the aggressor, and you will not be a passive victim.

6. Physically stop the attacker

Sometimes your only route to safety is to intervene physically to stop another person from doing harm. Of course the safest method in the long run is to avoid or prevent physical aggression, but that is not always possible. Perhaps you cannot retreat fast enough or your attempts to diffuse or dissuade an aggressor do not work. At such times, you will have to rely on your self defense skills to stop an attack. You will want to be far more effective and efficient a fighter than the predator ever imagined you to be. You will have to call up your trained physical capabilities, your knowledge of technique and strategy, and fiercely determined fighting spirit.

In a physical assault, your objective is to end the fight as quickly as possible and get yourself and others away from further danger. Ideally, you want fighting skills with techniques that are efficient, produce immediate results, render the attacker unable to continue the assault, and cut to the shortest time possible your need to be in contact with your assailant. You want to neutralize the assault quickly and decisively and get away to safety.

A self-defense situation is a far cry from a sports match. A brutal violent physical battle for life between human beings is not at all a thing of entertainment, sportsmanship, or "proving one's toughness." The knowledge and skills needed to win a street fight are very different from those needed to defeat a fellow athlete in a contest. Unseen knives are pulled from boot tops. Buddies or fellow gang members jump on a defender who thought he was fighting a single attacker. Gunfire blazes in what was thought to be a hand-to-hand shove-around fight.

Train honestly to be as prepared as possible. To develop reliable self protection skills, you must study under the guidance of mentors who understand the realities that make up the world of depraved humans who relish violence. A good teacher and an honest program will help keep your expectations and training exercises on target and authentic.

To-Shin Do self-defense training involves perfection of technique, choosing the right technique under pressure, and building the confidence to stand your ground.

Chapter Five

DEFENSE POSTURES
4 Progressing Stages
of Preparation

I f you were competing in a martial arts contest, you would assume an effective engagement stance immediately at the opening of the bout. You know why you are in the ring. You know why the other fighter is across from you. You are both intent on winning a fighting contest, and there is no ambiguity as to what your opponent's motives are.

Outside the ring is an entirely different reality. Most moments of most days of most good and happy people are focused on searching for and recognizing opportunities for benefit. Would you agree? We prefer to meet friends and allies. We do not enjoy unfriendly or unpredictable people. We seek out smiles and compliments. We avoid anger or insults. How about you? In most of your personal encounters in any given day, do you find more people likely to be pleasant and happy, or at least neutral, as opposed to confrontational or dangerous? Most healthy happy people prefer a party instead of an argument, a hug instead of a slug.

In a fighting contest, a bell rings and you know what happens next. On a sidewalk or in a parking lot, it might take a moment to recognize hostility. There may be no overt physical action at first; danger might begin to manifest with escalating language or even a wordless stare. We might question our perceptions or our feelings. Is this just a mouthy jerk, or is this a criminal setting up an assault? Is this just a grumpy loser having a bad day, or is this a psychotic about to pull a knife?

In the historical ninja warrior tradition I studied in Japan more than thirty years ago, part of the secrets the grandmaster shared with me was a set of *kamae* fighting postures for the outbreak of combat. But those historical fighting poses may not serve contemporary self defense needs in the best way today. Like the modern sport competitor in a consensual contest, the feudal Japanese warrior in a battle knew what the fighter across from him wanted to do. Like the competitor today, the warrior of yesterday was confronted with a declared fight from a designated enemy. Ninja or samurai, he took a strategic stance and used it to make the fight more difficult for his enemy.

But what of that vast gray area of uncertainty that characterizes unpredictable street assaults in modern civilian life? How do we train to prepare realistically? We cannot lift our fists and crouch into a martial arts movie pose every moment we suspect possible hostility. When and how do we learn effective ways to carry ourselves through the many days of peace and friendliness while we maintain readiness to recognize the moment of violence when it comes into being? In a world where so many martial arts focus on tactics of sport fighting in a consensual ring or imitating the movements of monks or soldiers consenting to battle in ancient Asia, where is the technology best suited for winning in the kinds of danger that threaten us in modern civilian life?

We must not be lulled into foolish smug confidence. We must avoid the false hope that by training to win in the ring or on the battlefield, we can easily win on the sidewalk or in the tavern as well. We need to train to prepare for protection of self and others in a foggy world where a battle could recede and disappear unexpectedly, or could just as likely explode into a life-altering moment of facing possible death.

We need a set of physical positions for protection that work in the world of laws, cultural norms, social expectations, and morals we inhabit today. We are not boxers in a ring. We are not commandos storming a beach. We are civilians in a community of enforced peace. As such, we need a set of progressing awareness steps that allow us to most efficiently gauge how far hostility has gone, how far it is likely to go, and where we need to be in all of that for best advantage. Therefore, rather than a set of different distinct postures for varying approaches to battle, for self-defense we practice a single progression of armoring and shielding that can increase or recede in intensity as a confrontation evolves from moment to moment.

1. NATURAL AT-EASE Shizen-tai
[pronounced *shee zen tah-ee*]

When it is clear you are in no danger of any possible hostility, you stand naturally at ease with your hands at your sides, fully open and totally secure. This is the way you stand in front of a beloved family member or friend or familiar work associate when there is no hint of any danger at all. Your body reflects the mental ease you feel with the situation at hand.

Begin your training in personal protection techniques with body awareness. Through heightened awareness of your body moving through space and time in relationship with other objects and bodies around you, you awaken your ability to sense your inner energy core and the fields of energy surrounding you. Is it possible that the way you interact with all the energies of any given encounter moment could make a situation more difficult for you, or conversely, put you more in command? Only when you are aware of how your body energy interacts with all that surrounds you can you begin to refine your ability to perceive what is taking place on many different levels during a possibly threatening encounter.

Developing such awareness begins with connecting to the earth. Stand firmly and naturally and feel the bottoms of both your feet in connection with the ground below. Is more weight on one foot than the other? Is more weight on the ball or heel of your feet? Is more weight on the inside or outside edge of each foot? Explore your foundation.

Now, feel the entire weight of your body sink down through the center of your feet, just behind the balls of your feet. Feel how your feet press into the ground. Feel as if you have roots sinking into the earth from the bottom of your feet. This is "grounding" yourself and becoming "rooted" in holding your position, standing your ground.

Practice feeling your feet solidly on the ground. Sink all your weight from the top of your head down through your torso along the front of your spinal column in the core of your body and finally through the center of your feet. Stabilize yourself in natural grounded dignity. Hold your place naturally with no need to assert your dominance or defend your position.

Remember to practice this upright grounded feeling often and at different times of day. Practice recognizing when it occurs naturally. Practice regaining it when you feel stressed, anxious, or overwhelmed. Practice holding it when you feel threatened internally or externally. Practice maintaining it when you are walking. Consciousness of your feet on the ground is a great way to let go of over-thinking and to get back to holding your ground naturally and solidly in your place on the planet.

2. ALERT AWARENESS

2.1

2.2

When you are unsure of your situation—*relatively* comfortable but a little on-alert based on another person's posture, movement, words, or facial expression—you naturally change your full open posture and allow a little cover and angling to give you an increased sense of comfort.

Pull one foot back slightly and stand at an easy angle with one foot forward. Raise your hands to hip level in front of you, palm-up or palm-down. You gesture lightly, moving your hands easily in the space between you and the other person, generating the slightest of barriers between the two of you.

No assault is likely to happen, but you nonetheless feel prompted to watch for possible awkwardness and maintain a slight safety buffer in front of you.

3. WARNING WARD-OFF

When you feel threatened with possible invasion—based on aggressively expressed motions or words from another person—you reposition to change your open posture and extend cover and increase angling to give you a greater sense of safety.

Step further back into an angled position with one foot forward. Your hands rise higher in front of you at the height of your throat and your

3.1

3.2

elbows are down to cover your ribs. Your palms are turned outward and your hands project like stop signs into the space between you and the other person.

You are strongly on alert for possible danger and you maintain an active safety buffer of distance and hands in front of you. You likely include the use of verbal statements to further create space to make it more difficult for the other person to get close, and you create effective positioning for directing and de-escalating the building tension.

4. DEFENSE READY *BO-BI GAMAE*
(pronounced *boh-bee gah-mah-eh*)

When it is clear that you will not be able to talk your way out or walk your way out of a hostile confrontation, set your body and awareness in *red alert mode* ready for immediate action.

Start with your left foot out front.

Your left toes aim forward and angle inward to your right just a little bit.

Your right foot is in the back.

Your right toes aim forward and angle outward to your right just a bit.

Side-to-side distance between the outside edge of your left foot and the outside edge of your right foot is the same distance as your hips are wide.

Front to back, your feet are about twice the distance as your hips are wide.

If you were on skis, and 12 o'clock was straight ahead, your skis would be aiming towards 1 o'clock while you were looking at 12 o'clock.

Flex your ankles, knees, and hips to lower your seat into a slightly crouching position.

Keep your back straight up with your shoulders over your hips. Do not stick your seat out behind. Do not hunch forward with your shoulders.

Tighten your abdominal muscles a little to strengthen your lower back and ready your body for action. In an actual confrontation, it will be very natural for your abdomen to tighten on its own.

Rock on your ankles and knees left and right and forward and back a little and find a just-right spot where you feel solid and yet ready to move into action.

If you were on a surfboard with a wave rolling beneath you, you would continuously flex and adjust just enough to stay coiled and responsive to a change in movement.

Lift both hands up with your left out in front of your right, lined up with the center of your throat.

Let your hands float so your finger tips are about as high as the tip of your nose.

Pull your elbows in and down in front of your ribs.

Keep your hands open and ready to deflect, or keep your front hand open and your rear hand balled into a fist.

4.1

4.2

Chapter Six

FIVE PHASES OF THE FIGHT

E ffective physical self defense and protection of others requires familiarity with a range of methods for all sorts of challenges. Sometimes you will need to get yourself or another person out from the grip of an aggressor who is using restraining techniques as his attack. In other situations you will do the opposite; you will need to catch and secure an aggressor with a subduing limb lock or choke. Sometimes you will need to shield yourself from an aggressor's blows. Other times you will be the one to use strategically precise strikes and kicks to stop an attacker's assault against you or another.

You want to command your physical body as a total unit capable of fitting into dangerous chaos effectively and applying the best actions to nullify an aggressor's attempts at dominance. It is not wise to separate techniques into classifications based on dynamics. Labeling training methods or entire arts with names like "stand-up fighting" or "kicking arts" or "close-up grappling throws" or "ground fighting" may work for marketing to imply some sort of special secrets offered by a given school of martial arts, but even that is debatable. Realistically, if your goal is effectively stopping aggression and protecting self and others outside of martial sport practice, you will need to be familiar with *all possibilities* an assailant might heap on you. You must let go of "partial arts."

"5 D" Problem-Solving Strategy

Regardless of the type of assault, you will find it valuable to recognize and acknowledge the value of a general pattern of five steps in any defense scenario. Once you actually begin practicing physical techniques for defending yourself against an attacker, your foundational strategy will follow these five distinct moments of purposeful decision-making to guide your physical action. Every self defense situation will pass through a similar set of stages in which you realize you are under attack, recognize what is going on, move to block or at least lessen the damage, and then stop more damage from coming in at you. We can call these five moments or phases of the fight the "5 Ds."

Discern – This is the first step to safety! To discern means to look carefully and see what is really there. Is there a problem coming your way? If there is, what exactly is it?

In self-defense, this means to stay aware enough to see a problem *before* it gets to you, and to see *exactly what* the problem truly is. This may have to happen very quickly, maybe in a heartbeat. On the other hand, this may happen in an agonizingly slow way as you struggle to figure out what some unpredictable person is about to do. Is this just a yapper, spitting out insults or threats as a way of impressing others or establishing some sort of status as a tough guy? Or is this a slapper, interviewing you for the role of victim, testing out your resolve or lack thereof to be sure that you will not resist effectively when he moves against you? If this is a person trying to hurt you, what does it look like he or she is going to do? Are they going to shove you? Hit you? Grab you? Take something away from you? Force you to go somewhere?

Based on what you see, get your mind and body in a position where you are ready to respond.

Defend – To defend means to keep the problem from hurting you. This is *step two* after seeing what the problem is. Do whatever you have to do *right away* to keep the problem from defeating you before you have a chance to take charge.

Timing can be challenging in a surprise attack. An assailant might fly at you completely unexpectedly, forcing you to discern and defend in what seems like the same instant.

What is the most effective and efficient way to keep the aggressor from being able to hurt you? If a person is still talking about what they intend to do to you, position yourself to be more difficult for a sudden hit or grab to reach, or get out of the area. If a person is shoving you, move with the push to escape. If a person is hitting you, move to position where you cannot be hit, or knock the hit away, or at least cover and protect the spot they are trying to hurt.

Disrupt – To disrupt means to do something to stop the problem from going where it wanted to go. In a next step beyond defense, you intervene with something to keep the problem from coming back at you again. You jam up the flow of the attacker's moves to defeat you.

Timing in disrupting application can vary. You may need more than one moment or action to thoroughly defend before going on to disrupt. In a most difficult challenge, you may have to discern, defend, and disrupt all in one moment where your disrupt is actually the defense.

If a person has tried to hit you, you might grab and twist their arm. If a person has grabbed you, you might hit or kick them in a spot they do not expect you to hit. If they try to wrestle you to the ground, you might shift and reposition your feet so they loose their balance and fall.

Deliver – To deliver means to take charge and make things go the way you want them to. Take over the problem in a way that makes the problem want to turn and run to get away from *you*.

Following a disrupt, you use your own counter-attack technique to knock down or throw back or lock up the person who tried to hurt you. This makes them have to defend. Having stopped the danger, you can get away to safety. You can restrain and hold them for arrest if that is appropriate. You can damage them to the point where they are incapable of further movement if that is necessary.

In a sports contest or a declared war, moving right away to the stage of delivering your attack against an opponent or an enemy may often be the best defense of all. You have already discerned why they are there in front of you, so why wait for them to get the jump on you first? As a police SWAT agent invading a stand-off, a military commando parachuting into battle, or a champion fighter defending a title, you are paid to start trouble and end it. There is no need or room for indecision. In a tense situation outside the ring or off the battlefield though, the deliver stage most often appears after the steps of recognizing and neutralizing the aggressor's initial move against you.

Discern – Remember that discern means to look carefully and see what is truly there. So, what do you have now? Are you safe? Is the problem *really* over? Or has the old problem turned into a *new problem* now?

If you have to defend yourself, this means you need to stay aware enough to see what problem might come up *next*. If a person has tried to hurt you and you knocked them away, will they run off, or will they come back at you again for a second try? The problem may not be over yet. Is more trouble on the way? If so, what kind of trouble this time?

Based on what you see, get your mind and body in a position where you are *ready for further response.*

In the fighting defense examples that follow in this volume, see if you can recognize the 5 D steps unfolding in the responses making up each technique string:

- ✦ In some cases, timing will be almost rhythmical; one move prompts the next.
- ✦ In other cases, the five steps may break into arrhythmical application; one move could generate many possible next steps.
- ✦ In some of the situations illustrated, the five steps may blur into each other and look like only three or even two steps.

Pacing and amount of time for each step will vary, based on what it takes to recognize the attack, and based on naturally expected emotional and physiological response patterns in people new to self-defense application training. Be honest with yourself. These techniques you will be practicing are not as easy as they look. Be patient with yourself. Build realistic confidence in your capabilities. The ability to fight off a dangerous person intent on damaging you is based on skill, and you can learn these skills.

Chapter Seven

FORWARD STRIKES AND KICKS AS PROTECTIVE MEASURES

When discussing self-defense and referring to the warrior discipline of historical Japanese *ninjutsu*, it is important to bear in mind that the ninja art is far broader than hand-to-hand combat alone. We need to understand the work of the people who came to be called *ninja*. In feudal Japan with its war after war between changing alliances of warlords, the ninja took a role as intelligence gatherer and psychological warfare expert. Historically, ninjutsu was the art of influencing others in ways that worked the ninja's will without those others having any knowledge that they were being influenced.

It is also likely in some cases that "ninja" was not a career identity, but more a description of work to be accomplished. Some serving in a ninja role might be lower level samurai warriors sent to blend in and observe a distant enemy or stir up dissent in the enemy's ranks. The job of the ninja involved gaining access to a place where information could be gathered, finding that information and verifying its reliability, and then getting out and reporting that information to a commander who could analyze it in light of related intelligence being reported back by others. It is most likely that some operating as ninja in the role of spy received little or no martial arts training at all.

Whether from a ninja family or taking a one-time role as ninja agent, some intelligence gatherers might have studied special combat arts with more emphasis on escaping a captor than charging into battle to defeat or capture an enemy. In ancient feudal Japan, ninja of the Togakure Ryu and ninja of the Momochi Sandayu family of Iga relied on practice of Koto Ryu koppo-jutsu for training in the ability to knock down an attacker in order to facilitate escape to safety. Koto Ryu koppo-jutsu was in those days a little-known skill in Japan, what might be called a trade secret martial technology. The Koto fighting style taught angular footwork that allowed a fighter to slip past an adversary's strike rather than block it, and then damage the exposed limb with punishing strikes.

In the classical ninja taijutsu unarmed defense methods I studied in Japan, knock-down hits were referred to as *koppo-jutsu* 骨法術. The *ko* 骨 of the Japanese word *koppo* translates as "bone," implying body frame. *Po* of *koppo* is a way of pronouncing *ho* 法, which translates as "law" or principles by which something is reliably done. *Jutsu* 術 is "art" or science. In ninja taijutsu practice, the essence of *koppo-jutsu* is your body frame moving and generating momentum to damage the bones or unbalance the adversary's frame to gain dominance over him in a fight.

The Togakure ninja's Koto Ryu koppo-jutsu method featured a closed balled-up fist that was distinctly Chinese in origin and very uncharacteristic of the unarmed fighting of Japan five hundred years ago. 1800s-born Togakure Ryu master Toshitsugu Takamatsu often called this Koto Ryu technology *koppo karate* 骨法唐手. The Japanese *kara* 唐 referred to old China, and *te* 手 is translated as "hand," giving us the term "traditional Chinese hand-to-hand fighting."

In our contemporary world, effective striking techniques are an important part of your defense skills. As a trained protector, you may have to knock an aggressor back away from a person you are shielding, or even stun a attacker into reduced consciousness so you can force safety and peace into the situation. It is also possible that you may need to use impact against an inanimate object to rescue or protect someone; you may need to kick in a door, knock out a window, or drive back some obstacle.

For those learning foundational self-defense in a world where we might not have years to condition our bodies as weapons, it might be best to start training in impact techniques using the base of the open hand palm rather than the *koppo-jutsu* balled-up fist. The tight fist driving forward on the end of the forearm is a skill that takes some time to master. Consistent proper bone alignment needs to be developed. Timing of the punch extension in relation to the rest of the body needs to be developed. Strong wrists and perfect angling need to be developed. In the first stages of training, it may be more appropriate for effective self-defense to replace the fist with an open palm. At the same time, you can begin to cultivate a strong fist in training so that it will be available later after some months of practice.

LESSON 1 PART 1

The Cross Punch Strike

As a trained protector, you will need to know how to throw a rock solid knock-back or knock-down strike with your rear positioned arm. In To-Shin Do taijutsu unarmed defender training, we call this a ***cross punch***. Your right arm crosses over your chest from your rear shoulder to hit a target in front of you.

1. Start in left-forward Defense Ready *Bo-bi Gamae* "ready to defend" fighting posture with your left foot forward and right foot in back.

2. To throw the strike, you do three things at the exact same moment:

    a) Rock forward over your left foot—do not step; just rock, or maybe at most shift your left foot forward an inch or two

    b) Twist across your shoulders so your right shoulder moves forward and your left shoulder pulls back—remember to keep your shoulders over your hips; do not lean your upper body forward

    c) Straighten your right arm so your right palm heel (base of your palm just above your wrist) drives forward into the target - let

your wrist, elbow, and shoulder align so the bones are in line behind the straight forward pressure of your strike (avoid lifting your
shoulder up or angling your elbow out or making impact with
your wrist coming in at an angle).

3. Penetrate the target with a deep straight thrust to move the target backwards with your impact. Do not just pop the target and pull
your hand back. Later in more advanced phases of your training, you
will practice using a cross punch as a convincing feint to distract the

aggressor, allowing you to follow with low kicks, but for now just concentrate on a firm penetrating strike.

4. Once the strike has pushed the target backwards, pull your right hand straight back to its original position. Do not swing your hand through the target or drop your hand down to pull it back—pull it back through the same straight line path it took to fly forward into the target.

Try the same technique with your right foot forward and your left shoulder towards the rear—throw a left arm cross punch strike.

LESSON 1 PART 2

Defense Against a Cross Punch Strike Attack

What if someone uses this great rescue technique as an aggressive attack to assault you? If an aggressor throws a cross punch angling in at your face or head, you need to know how to defend right away and then disrupt and stop the assault and finally prevent the aggressor from continuing against you.

In To-Shin Do Taijutsu unarmed defender training, we call this practice exercise *"Ko-yoku"* - **earth grounded hand-edge defense inside a hooking thrust, finished with knock-back strikes up the centerline.**

1. Start in any of the four natural confrontation preparation postures, with a gap of just a bit further than one extended arm length between the center of your chest and the center of the attacker's chest.

2. Attacker shifts his left foot forward and swings a high right punch, or shove, or grab around and in from your left side, aiming for your head or neck.

3. Sink to stabilize yourself on flexed knees, raise your hands up your body's center line, and at the top of the rise, drive your left hand edge up and out to hit the inside of the attacker's right arm to stop his cross punch. To be sure you breathe powerfully and do not accidentally suck your breath in, shout a growling command *Stop it!* as you hit his arm.

4. Continue to cover with your upraised left arm, and drive a right palm heel strike upwards under his chin to knock his head back, or drive your

right hand edge up and forward into the right side of his throat, one or two times, shouting the growled *Stop it!* command with each strike.

5. Shift towards his right punching arm with your left forearm covering the left side of your head, grab his right shoulder to stabilize yourself, and then drive your right knee into his thighs, groin, and abdomen one, two, or three times, shouting the growled command *Stop it!* with each strike.

5.1

5.2

5.3

6. As the attacker collapses, step backwards with your right foot and strike down on his right ear or temple with your left palm heel one or two times to push him away, shouting the command *Stop it!* with each strike.

7. Lower your hips and shove him away with a loud command of *Back off!* Keep your eyes on the attacker as you assume an alert left-forward Defense Ready position. Watch for possible follow-up attacks from the original assailant or from his friends, and then get away to a safe place as quickly as you can.

Try the same technique against an attacker's left cross punch strike to the right side of your head, using your right hand to defend, left palm to counter strike, and left knee to counter attack, right hand finishing blow, and escape to a right-forward Defense Ready position.

6.1

6.2

7.1

7.2

LESSON 1 PART 3

Cross Punch Strike Defense - Target Drill

Use a target pad drill version of the series to develop power, accuracy, timing, and balance in movement as you practice the techniques of the defense. A trainer holds a firm target pad strapped to his palm and forearm to give you a safe striking surface you can hit with full power.

1. Start in any of the four natural confrontation preparation postures, with a gap of just a bit further than one extended arm length between the center of your chest and the center of the attacker's chest.

2. Trainer shifts his left foot forward and swings a high right target pad slap around and in from your left side, aiming for the left side of your head.

3. Stabilize yourself on flexed knees, raise your hands up your body's center line, and at the top of the rise, drive your left hand edge up and out to hit the inside of the trainer's right arm target pad. Shout the command *Stop it!* as you hit the target pad.

4. Trainer shifts to his left and turns to his right to a position with his right arm lifted with target stretched forward perpendicular to your path.

5. Continue to cover with your upraised left arm, and drive a right palm heel strike forward into the target in front of you one or two times, shouting the command *Stop it!* with each strike into the target pad.

6. Trainer rotates his right arm and aims the target pad downwards and then supports the target from above with his left hand.

7. Grab the top of the target pad and pull it down into your rising right knee strikes, shouting the command *Stop it!* with each strike into the target.

8. Trainer rotates his right arm inward, lifts and bends his right elbow, and supports the target with his left hand on the straps in position with the pad striking surface pointing away from him.

9. Step backwards with your right foot and strike down and across to the target pad with your left palm heel, shouting the command *Back off!* Keep your eyes on the trainer as you assume left-forward Defense Ready.

LESSON 2 PART 1

Leading-Hand Strike

As a trained protector, you will need to know how to throw a quick but solid knock-back or stunning strike with your leading arm. In To-Shin Do taijutsu unarmed defender training, we call this a ***leading-hand strike.*** It flies straight out from your leading arm to hit a target in front of you.

1. Start in left-forward Defense Ready *Bo-bi Gamae* "ready to defend" fighting posture with your left foot forward and right foot in back.

2. To throw the strike, you do three things at the *exact same moment*:

- Rock forward over your left foot—do not step; just rock, or maybe at most shift your left foot forward an inch or two
- Twist your left shoulder inward so your left shoulder moves forward and your right shoulder pulls back—remember to keep your shoulders over your hips; do not lean your upper body forward
- Straighten your left arm so your left palm heel (base of your palm just above your wrist) drives forward into the target—let your wrist, elbow, and shoulder align so the bones are in line behind the straight forward pressure of your strike (avoid lifting your shoulder up or angling your elbow out or making impact with your wrist coming in at an angle).

3. Penetrate the target with a deep straight thrust to move the target backwards with your impact. Do not just pop the target and pull your hand back. Later in more advanced phases of your training, you will practice using a leading hand strike as a darting fingertip spear to the eyes to force an aggressor to flinch away or reposition, allowing you to follow with power hits, but for now just concentrate on a quick solid strike.

4. Once the strike has pushed the target backwards, drop your elbow straight down to pull your left hand straight back to its original position.

Do not swing your hand through the target or drop your hand down to pull it back—pull it back through the same straight line path it took to fly forward into the target.

Try the same technique with your right foot forward and your left shoulder towards the rear—throw a left arm leading-hand punch strike.

LESSON 2 PART 2

Defense Against a Leading-Hand Strike Attack

What if someone uses this great rescue technique as an aggressive attack to assault you? If an aggressor throws a straight-in leading-hand punch at your face, you need to know how to defend right away and then disrupt and stop the assault and finally prevent the aggressor from continuing against you.

In To-Shin Do Taijutsu unarmed defender training, we call this practice exercise *"Yoku-to"* **- earth grounded palm deflect defense** *outside* **a straight thrust, finished with knock-away strikes from outside the centerline.**

1. Start in any of the four natural confrontation preparation postures, with a gap of just a bit further than one extended arm length between the center of your chest and the center of the attacker's chest.

2. Attacker shifts his right foot forward and throws a high right punch, or shove, or grab straight in to your center, aiming for your head or neck.

3. Sink to stabilize yourself on flexed knees, raise your hands up your body's center line, and at the top of the rise, drive your left palm up and in to hit the outside of the attacker's right arm to deflect his leading-hand punch. To be sure you breathe powerfully and do not accidentally suck your breath in, shout a growling command *Stop it!* as you hit his arm.

4. Continue to press with your extended left arm, and drive a right palm heel strike across to his right temple to knock his head back, or drive your right palm heel or hand edge into his right ribs beneath his extended right arm, one or two times, shouting the growled *Stop it!* command with each strike.

5. Shift left around his right punching arm with your left palm pressing his right shoulder and right palm grabbing or pressing his right upper arm to stabilize yourself, and then drive your right knee into the side of his right thigh near his hip, one, two, or three times, shouting the growled command *Stop it!* with each strike.

6. As the attacker reacts, step further left with your right and then left foot to end up behind him. Grab his shoulders to keep him facing forward, and then drive your left knee up into the base of his tailbone with full power strikes, one, two, or three times, shouting the growled command *Stop it!* with each strike.

7. Lower your hips and shove him away with a loud command of *Back off!* Keep your eyes on the attacker as you assume an alert left-forward Defense Ready position. Watch for possible follow-up attacks from the original assailant or from his friends, and then get away to a safe place as quickly as you can.

Try the same technique against an attacker's left leading-hand punch strike to the center of your head, using your right hand to defend, left palm to counter strike, left knee to counter attack, and right knee finishing blow, and escape to a right-forward Defense Ready position.

LESSON 2 PART 3

Leading-Hand Strike Defense - Target Drill

Use a target pad drill version of the series to develop power, accuracy, timing, and balance in movement as you practice the techniques of the defense. A trainer holds a firm target pad strapped to the back of his right hand and another target strapped to his left palm to give you a safe striking surface you can hit with full power.

1. Start in any of the four natural confrontation preparation postures, with a gap of just a bit further than one extended arm length between the center of your chest and the center of the attacker's chest.

2. Trainer rotates his right arm inward and supports the target with his left hand on the straps in position with the pad striking surface pointing away from him, and then shifts his right foot forward and pushes a high right target pad edge into your center line, aiming for the center of your head or chest.

3. Stabilize yourself on flexed knees, raise your hands up your body's center line, and at the top of the rise, drive your left hand palm up and in to hit the outside of the trainer's right arm target pad. Shout the command *Stop it!* as you hit the target pad.

4. Trainer shifts to his left and lifts his left hand to a position with his right arm lifted with target stretched forward perpendicular to your path.

5. Continue to cover with your upraised left palm, and drive a right palm heel strike forward into the target in front of you one or two times, shouting the command *Stop it!* with each strike into the target pad.

6. Trainer lowers and twists his right arm to aim the target pad outwards and then supports the target from behind with his left hand.

7. Hold the trainer's right shoulder and upper arm and drive your rising right knee strikes into the target pad, shouting the command *Stop it!* with each strike into the target.

8. Trainer steps left and around with his left foot and supports the target with his left hand on the straps in position with the pad striking surface pointing down.

9. Plant your right foot and rotate left, and then drive your rising left knee strikes into the target pad, shouting the command *Stop it!*

10. Trainer lifts and supports the target with his left hand on the straps in position with the pad striking surface pointing away from him.

11. Step backwards with your right foot and strike forward into the target pad with your left palm heel, shouting the command *Back off!* Keep your eyes on the trainer as you assume left-forward Defense Ready.

LESSON 3 PART 1

Forward Driving Kick

As a trained protector, you will need to know how to throw a solid drive through or knock-down kick with your rear positioned leg. In To-Shin Do taijutsu unarmed defender training, we call this a ***front kick.*** With your left foot forward, your right leg swings up and out to hit a target in front of you.

1. Start in left-forward Defense Ready *Bo-bi Gamae* "ready to defend" fighting posture with your left foot forward and right foot in back.

2. To throw the strike, you do three things at the *exact same moment*:

   • Rock forward over your left foot—do not step; just rock, or maybe at most shift your left foot forward an inch or two

   • Twist across your shoulders so your right shoulder moves forward and your left shoulder pulls back—remember to keep your shoulders over your hips; do not lean your upper body forward

   • Lift your right knee high and push forward to drive the bottom of your right heel into the target—let your ankle, knee, and hip align so the bones are in line behind the straight forward pressure of your strike (avoid lifting your shoulder up or angling your elbow out or making impact with your wrist coming in at an angle).

3. Sink to stabilize yourself on flexed knees and raised your hands up your body's center line for balance and protective cover. Lift your left knee and drive the bottom of your left heel and sole down and forward to hit the front of the attacker's right shin or knee. Twist your left hip and your left foot outward to provide more foot surface to stop the attacker's leg. To be sure you breathe powerfully and do not accidentally suck your breath in, shout a growling command *Stop it!* as you kick his leg.

4. Once the kick has pushed the target backwards, pull your foot back slightly and put your right foot straight down on the ground in a new forward position.

Try the same technique with your right foot forward and your left shoulder towards the rear—throw a left leg front kick.

LESSON 3 PART 2

Defense Against a Forward Driving Kick Attack

What if someone uses this great rescue technique as an aggressive attack to assault you? If an aggressor throws a forward driving kick at your leg or groin, you need to know how to defend right away and then disrupt and stop the assault and finally prevent the aggressor from continuing against you.

In To-Shin Do Taijutsu unarmed defender training, we call this practice exercise *"Hi-cho"* **Earth ground-holding; stamp-kick down to rising swing kick.**

1. Start in any of the four natural confrontation preparation postures, with a gap of a bit further than one extended arm length between the center of your chest and the center of the attacker's chest.

2. Attacker shifts his left foot forward and throws a right front kick, aiming for your left leg or groin.

3. Sink to stabilize yourself on flexed knees and raise your hands up your body's center line for balance and protective cover. Lift your left knee and drive the bottom of your left heel and sole down and forward to hit the front of the attacker's right shin or knee. Twist your left hip and your left foot inward to provide more foot surface to stop the attacker's

leg. To be sure you breathe powerfully and do not accidentally suck your breath in, shout a growling command *Stop it!* as you kick his leg.

4. Continue to cover with your upraised left arm, and drive a right palm heel strike forward to his forehead to knock his head back, shouting the growled *Stop it!* command with the strike. (In a real attack, your hard kick to the attacker's leg will most likely cause his upper body to pitch forward as he retracts his leg in pain. That is why you then throw a right palm strike to his face. Be sure your training partner knows how to imitate realistically this physiological reaction with his leg so training reflects reality. *If the attacker does fall back* from your kick to his leg rather than pitch forward, skip this step 4 palm strike and follow right away with step 5 kick to his leg or groin.)

5. Shift forward with your left foot and either drive your right foot into his knee, thigh, or abdomen, or swing your right shin or boot toe up

between his thighs to his groin, shouting the growled command *Stop it!* with the strike.

6. As the attacker collapses, step forward with your right foot and shove both of your palms forward to strike the attacker's face or shoulders and push him away, with a loud command of *Back off!* Keep your eyes on the attacker as you assume alert left-forward Defense Ready position. Watch for possible follow-up attacks from the original assailant or from his friends, and then get away to a safe place as quickly as you can.

Try the same technique against an attacker's left front kick to your right leg, using your right foot to defend, left palm to counter strike, and left kick to counter attack, right hand finishing blow, and escape to a right-forward Defense Ready position.

LESSON 3 PART 3

Forward Driving Kick Defense - Target Drill

Use a target pad drill version of the series to develop power, accuracy, timing, and balance in movement as you practice the techniques of the defense. A trainer holds a firm target pad strapped to his palm and forearm to give you a safe striking surface you can hit with full power.

1. Start in any of the four natural confrontation preparation postures, with a gap of just a bit further than one extended arm length between the center of your chest and the center of the attacker's chest.

2. Trainer crouches very low as he shifts his left foot forward and swings a low right target pad up and forward from his right knee, almost like a bowler's swing, aiming for your left knee.

3. Stabilize yourself on flexed knees, raise your hands up your body's center line, and at the top of the rise, drive your left foot straight into the trainer's moving target pad. Shout the command *Stop it!* as you kick the target pad.

4. Trainer lifts the target up to where it faces you in your path.

5. Continue to cover with your upraised left arm, and drive a right palm heel strike forward into the target in front of you one or two times, shouting the command *Stop it!* with each strike into the target pad.

6. Trainer lowers the target and aims it upward slightly (to receive the stamping front kick), or rotates his right arm to aims the target pad downwards and supports the target from above with his left hand (to receive the upward swinging groin kick).

7. Drive your right foot forward or swing your right shin upward into the target, shouting the command *Stop it!* with each kick into the target.

8. Trainer lifts his right arm with the pad striking surface aiming at you.

9. Step forward with your right foot and strike into the target pad with both palm heels, shouting the command *Back off!* Keep your eyes on the trainer as you assume left-forward Defense Ready.

Chapter Eight

FRONT ARM CAPTURES AND RESTRAINTS

The ninjutsu of Japanese history was a system for gaining information to influence wars and plan battles. This means that ninjutsu was a discipline covering study of far more than just a martial art of fighting techniques. Not all ninja were combat experts. Some ninja agents likely had little martial arts training, and their value was being at the right place at the right time with access to the right person. On the other hand, some ninja trained to become highly capable fighters.

What I traveled to Japan to study specifically were the martial arts taught to those who carried out ninjutsu intelligence gathering. Additionally, my teacher also taught me martial systems developed for more conventional battles not necessarily restricted to ninja intelligence gathering activities. Along with arts like the Togakure and Iga ninja's Koto Ryu koppo-jutsu, I learned as well Takagi Yoshin Ryu classical warrior unarmed defense. The grappling, throwing, and joint locking that characterizes Takagi Yoshin Ryu is referred to as *ju-tai-jutsu* 柔体術. *Ju* 柔 in Japanese translates as the familiar "supple" of the *ju* of judo. *Tai* 体 translates as "body." Jutsu 術 is "art" or science.

In our contemporary world, effective grab and grapple counters are an important part of your protector skills. When protecting another or yourself from attack, you may have to grab and secure an aggressor's arm or wrist to keep him from hitting or grabbing, or to prevent or interrupt him from drawing a weapon. It is also possible that you may need to use an equally quick, direct, and powerful grasp to secure an inanimate object in order to rescue or protect someone; you may need to grab a falling pole, secure a swinging door, or catch some object flying at you.

In the first months of learning foundational self-defense, practice conditioning your hands and forearms to develop a firm grip. Be sure that your body is in the proper place so that distancing and angling can work to your advantage. For a little while, you might have to step and then grip. After some practice, you can begin to develop the skill of grasping—or countering an aggressor's grasp—at the same moment you move into best position.

LESSON 4 PART 1

Cross Grab as a Rescue

As a trained defender, you will need to know how to step forward quickly and reach across your body to secure an attacker's arm with precision and strength. In To-Shin Do taijutsu unarmed defender training, we call this a **cross grab.** Your arm crosses over your chest to grab a target in front of you. If these are human aggressors, your right hand grasps their right arm, or your left hand grasps their left.

1. Start in left-forward Defense Ready *Bo-bi Gamae* "ready to defend" fighting posture with your left foot forward and right foot in back. The

aggressor steps across in front of you and threatens to hit, shove or grab your friend with his right hand, leaving you in a position outside the aggressor's right arm.

2. To secure the grab, you do three things at the exact same moment:

- Rock forward over your left foot—do not step; just rock, or maybe at most shift your left foot forward an inch or two

- Twist across your shoulders so your right shoulder moves forward and your left shoulder pulls back—remember to keep your shoulders over your hips; do not lean your upper body forward

- Straighten your right arm so your right hand reaches for the aggressor's right wrist with your right palm down and your right thumb pointing away from you. (Do not reach in with your palm coming up from beneath their arm with your thumb pointing out at you.)

3. Push your right palm into his right wrist with firm pressure to facilitate a tight grasp. Do not just try to catch with your fingers. Later in more advanced phases of training, you will practice grabbing with fingertip pressure on nerve points to cause pain and distract the aggressor, but for now just concentrate on a firm controlling grasp.

4. Once you have gripped the aggressor's right wrist with your right hand, pull his right hand out and down as you step back with your right leg. Press the back of his right arm with your upraised left arm to help

unbalance him when he resists your grip. Shout a growling command *Stop it!* as you pull out and press down on his arm.

5. Turn to your right and use shuffling footwork with flexing knees to pull the aggressor down and away from the person you are rescuing. Pull towards you and press down as you back up to keep the aggressor off balance. Avoid staying in place and trying to wrestle the aggressor down with crude arm strength as he moves to regain his leverage.

Try the same technique with your right foot forward and your left shoulder towards the rear—reach out with a left arm cross grab to his left wrist.

LESSON 4 PART 2

Defense Against a Cross Grab Attack

What if someone uses a strong and precise grab as an aggressive attack to pin down your arm? If an aggressor reaches across to grasp your wrist or arm, you need to know how to defend right away and then disrupt and stop the assault and finally escape or reverse the grab to keep the aggressor from dominating you.

In To-Shin Do taijutsu unarmed defender training, we call this practice exercise *"Te-hodoki 3"* **Forward-facing cross-side grab escape (his right to your right).**

1. Start in a guarded confrontation preparation posture with your hands low in front of you in alert position, with a gap of just a bit further than one extended arm length between the center of your chest and the center of the attacker's chest.

2. Attacker steps forward with his right foot and grabs your right wrist or forearm with his right hand. His right palm is on the top of your arm and his thumb points away from him.

3. Sink to stabilize yourself on flexed knees, being aware that he might try to hit you with his free left hand. As you sink to stabilize yourself, you may even move to your left to move away from his left hand.

4. Give a tug on your trapped right arm as though to pull it out of the aggressor's right grasp, and then abruptly sink further on flexed knees and shove your trapped arm forward and down to jam into his grip. The sudden change in direction of tension can cause your arm to pop out of

the aggressor's grip as he concentrates on believing he is preventing you from pulling your arm backwards and out.

5. If the attacker is still holding on to your arm, hammer down on his right forearm with the bottom of your left fist, or punch your left hand into the bones of the back of his right hand as you pull your right arm free. Be sure you breathe powerfully and do not accidentally suck your breath in. Shout a growling command *Stop it!* as you hit his arm or hand.

6. Once you are free, lift both arms up in a shielding position with your elbows low and palms aimed out, and kick the toe or heel of your right foot into the attacker's right ankle or shin, one, two, or three times, shouting the growled *Stop it!* command with each kick.

7. As the attacker collapses away from your kicks, lower your hips and shove him away with a loud command of *Back off!* Keep your eyes on the attacker as you assume an alert left-forward Defense Ready position.

7.1   7.2

Watch for possible follow-up attacks from the original assailant or from his friends, and then get away to a safe place as quickly as you can.

Try the same technique against an attacker's left cross grab to your left arm, using your right hand to strike down on his left forearm or hand, and left knee to counter attack, right hand finishing blow, and escape to a right-forward Defense Ready position.

LESSON 4 PART 3

Cross Grab Escaping Defense - Target Drill

Use a target pad drill version of the series to develop power, accuracy, timing, and balance in movement as you practice the techniques of the escape. A trainer holds a firm target pad strapped to the back of his right hand to give you a safe striking surface you can hit with full power. (Though not illustrated here, he could also hold with his left hand an upright tall body bag target for your kicks.)

1. Start in a guarded confrontation preparation posture with your hands low in front of you in alert position, with a gap of just a bit further than one extended arm length between the center of your chest and the center of the attacker's chest.

2. Trainer wearing a striking pad on the back of his right hand shifts his left foot forward and grabs your right wrist.

2

4.1

4.2

3. Stabilize yourself on flexed knees, and push down and forward abruptly to see if you can push your right arm out of the trainer's right grip.

4. If his grip persists, raise your left hand and then hit down with a full-body hammer strike or knuckle punch to the pad on the back of the trainer's right hand. Shout the command *Stop it!* as you hit the target pad.

5. If his grip still persists, pull your left hand to your right shoulder and then hit down with a full-body hammer fist or hand-edge strike to the pad on the back of the trainer's right hand. Shout the command *Stop it!* as you hit the target pad and pull your right arm free.

4.3

4.4

6. Raise your arms to cover as you move to your left. Though not illustrated here, you could kick a target standing in front of you two or three times with the toe or heel of your right foot, shouting the command *Stop it!* with each kick, and then step backwards with the command *Back off!* while keeping your eyes on the trainer.

LESSON 5 PART 1

Mirror-Side Grab as a Rescue

As a trained defender, you will need to know how to step forward quickly and reach straight out to secure an attacker's arm with precision

and strength. In To-Shin Do taijutsu unarmed defender training, we call this a ***mirror-side grab.*** Your arm reaches forward to grab a target in front of you, as though grabbing an object in a mirror reflection. If these are human aggressors, your right hand grasps their left arm, or your left hand grasps their right.

1. Start in *Shizen* natural posture with your left foot forward and right foot in back. The aggressor steps into position in front of you and pulls out a weapon with his right hand, leaving you in a position shielding a friend behind you.

2. To secure the grab, you do three things at the *exact same moment*:
   - Step forward with your left foot
   - Twist your left shoulder inward so your left shoulder moves forward and your right shoulder pulls back—remember to keep your shoulders over your hips; do not lean your upper body forward
   - Straighten your left arm so your left hand reaches for the aggressor's right wrist with your left palm down and your left thumb pointing away from you. (Do not reach in with your palm coming up from beneath their arm with your thumb pointing back at you.)

3. Push your left palm into his right wrist with firm pressure to facilitate a tight grasp. Do not just try to catch with your fingers. Later in more advanced phases of training, you will practice grabbing with directional pressure to cause the aggressor's balance to be compromised, but for now just concentrate on a firm controlling grasp.

4. Once you have gripped the aggressor's right wrist with your left hand, push his right hand out and back as you step further forward with your left leg. Strike with your upraised right palm to help unbalance him when he resists your grip. Shout a growling command *Stop it!* as you pull out and press down on his arm.

5. Turn to your left with flexing knees and use your right heel behind the aggressor's right heel to trip him and pull him down backwards to his seat, away from the person you are rescuing. Step forward and to the side to go behind the aggressor and keep him off balance. Avoid staying in place and trying to wrestle the aggressor down with crude leg swings as he moves to regain his leverage.

Try the same technique with your right foot forward and your left shoulder towards the rear—reach out with a right arm mirror-side grab to his left wrist.

LESSON 5 PART 2

Defense Against a Mirror-Side Grab Attack

What if someone uses their strong and precise mirror-side grab as an aggressive attack to pin down your arm? If an aggressor reaches forward to grasp your wrist or arm, you need to know how to defend right away and then disrupt and stop the assault and finally escape or reverse the grab to keep the aggressor from dominating you.

In To-Shin Do taijutsu unarmed defender training, we call this practice exercise *"Dan-shu"* **Mirror-side grab defense (his left to your right).**

1. Start in a guarded confrontation preparation posture with your hands low in front of you in alert position, with a gap of just a bit further than one extended arm length between the center of your chest and the center of the attacker's chest.

2. Attacker steps forward with his left foot and grabs your right wrist or forearm with his left hand. His left palm is on the top of your arm and his thumb points away from him.

3. Sink to stabilize yourself on flexed knees, being aware that he might try to hit you or shove you back with his free right hand. As you sink to stabilize yourself, you may even move to your right to move away from his right hand.

4. Swing both hands up along your body center line, opening your hands to where they rise upward with palms facing each other. The back of your left hand may bump the attacker's right hand away from inside, and the back of your right hand will invert and weaken the aggressor's left hand grip to where your right hand slips out of his grasp.

5. Use the bottoms of both fists to hammer down on his left arm, collarbone, or bridge of the nose. Be sure you breathe powerfully and do not accidentally suck your breath in. Shout a growling command *Stop it!* as you strike down with your fists.

6. From position inside the aggressor's arms, hold onto his left shoulder and neck to stabilize your balance, and then swing your left knee forward and up with strikes to his thigh or groin one, two, or three times, shouting the growled *Stop it!* command with each strike.

7. As the attacker collapses away from your knee strikes, lower your hips and shove him away with a loud command of *Back off!* In future advanced training, you will practice locking up and pinning down the aggressor to restrain him from further attack, but for now just concentrate on getting free so that you can escape. Keep your eyes on the attacker as you assume an alert left-forward Defense Ready position. Watch for possible

6.1

6.2

6.3   6.4

follow-up attacks from the original assailant or from his friends, and then get away to a safe place as quickly as you can.

Try the same technique against an attacker's right mirror-side grab to your left arm, using both hands to strike down on his right arm and collarbone, and right knee to counter attack, right hand finishing blow, and escape to a right-forward Defense Ready position.

7

LESSON 5 PART 3

Mirror-Side Grab Escaping Defense - Target Drill

Use a target pad drill version of the exercise to develop power, accuracy, timing, and balance in movement as you practice the techniques of escaping a mirror-side limb grab. A trainer holds a firm target pad strapped to his right hand to give you a safe striking surface you can hit with full power.

1. Start in a guarded confrontation preparation posture with your hands low in front of you in alert position, with a gap of just a bit further than one extended arm length between the center of your chest and the center of the attacker's chest.

2. Trainer wears a striking pad on the inside of his right forearm, and steps forward with his left foot and grabs your right arm.

3. Stabilize yourself on flexed knees, and lift both hands up abruptly to pull your right arm out of the trainer's left grip.

4. With your hands raised from the grip escape, hammer down into the pad on the inside of the trainer's right arm. Shout the command *Stop it!* as you hit the target pad.

6.1

6.2

6.3

5. Trainer lowers both arms to position where his arms hold the target pad downwards supported from above with both hands. Drive your left knee up into the target two or three times, shouting the command *Stop it!* with each knee to the target.

6. Drive forward to push the trainer away with palm shove strikes. Though not illustrated here, you could follow up with kicks to the lowered target, shouting the command *Back off!* Keep your eyes on the trainer as you assume left-forward Defense Ready.

LESSON 6 PART 1

Double Wrist Grab as a Rescue

As a trained defender, you will need to know how to step forward quickly and reach straight out to secure both an attacker's arms with precision and strength. In To-Shin Do taijutsu unarmed defender training, we call this an ***upright double wrist grab.*** Your arms reach forward to grab two targets in front of you, as though grabbing in a mirror

reflection. If this is a human aggressor, your right hand grasps the left arm and your left hand grasps the right.

1. Start in left-forward Defense Ready *Bo-bi Gamae* "ready to defend" fighting posture with your left foot forward and right foot in back. The aggressor steps into position in front of you and lunges in with both hands to grab and grapple with you as you shield a friend behind you.

2. To secure the grab, you do three things at the *exact same moment*:

   • Flex your knees deeply to drop lower than he expects you to be.
   • Step forward and grap his wrists from below—remember to keep your shoulders over your hips; do not lean your upper body forward.

• Use rising action on your legs to secure him in place with your double grip. Push your left palm in beneath his right wrist with your left thumb pointing towards his fingers. At the same instant, grip his left wrist with your right with your right thumb pointing towards his fingers.

3. Holding the aggressor's wrists in place, lift your right knee high and drive your right heel sharply into his left hip to fold him over. Shout a growling command *Stop it!* as you kick your heel into his hip to knock him off balance.

4. Angle your right foot out so that the heel fits the fold of his hip for solid impact.

5. Pull your right leg back and then swing your right knee upward to strike him one or two times under the chin or to the side of his face.

Try the same technique with your right foot forward and your left shoulder towards the rear, and kick with your left heel to his right hip once you have secured the double wrist grab.

LESSON 6 PART 2

Defense Against a Double Wrist Grab Attack

An aggressor could use this upright double wrist grab to restrain both your arms, and this defensive rescue could then become an assault. If an aggressor reaches forward to grasp both your wrists, you need to know how to defend right away and then disrupt and stop the assault and finally escape or reverse the grab to keep the aggressor from dominating you.

In To-Shin Do taijutsu unarmed defender training, we call this practice exercise *"Te-Hodoki 1"* **Upright double wrist grab escape defense**.

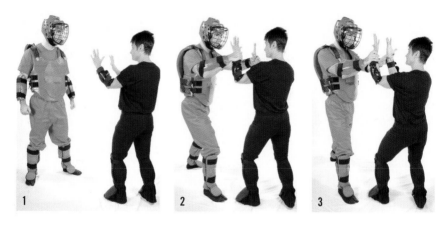

1. Start in a guarded confrontation preparation posture with your hands held up in warding off position, with a gap of just a bit further than one extended arm length between the center of your chest and the center of the attacker's chest.

2. Attacker steps forward with his right foot and grabs both your wrists, one in each of his hands. His palms are on the underside of your arms and his thumbs point towards your fingers.

3. Sink to stabilize yourself on flexed knees, and take note of how he is using his arms to hold you in place. Does he hold your wrists close together and push them into the center of your chest? Or does he pull your wrists apart to open up your center?

4. If the aggressor holds your wrists high and close to each other, rotate your wrists to where you can see your palms and then slam your two wrists towards each other sharply two or three times to bang together the aggressor's two thumbs.

5. Pull back with your right leg, and slice the outer edges of your palms down with a scissor action to knock his stunned hands off your wrists.

6. Be sure you breathe powerfully to build and release your energy and prevent accidentally sucking your breath in. Shout a growling command *Stop it!* each time you bang his thumbs together and when you shear his hands away.

7. If the aggressor does the opposite and holds your wrists far apart, sink your seat low, as though trying to pull away, and then suddenly lurch forward with a forehead ram up into his chin or lips and nose one or two times to stun him.

8. Swing your right shin up to his groin once or twice and then use the bottom of your right foot to push him away.

9. Again, breathe powerfully to build and release your energy and prevent accidentally sucking your breath in. Shout a growling command *Stop it!* each time you ram his face with your head and kick to his body.

10. As the attacker collapses away from your knee strikes, lower your hips and shove him away with a loud command of *Back off!* In future advanced training, you will practice locking up and pinning down the aggressor to restrain him from further attack, but for now just concentrate

on getting free so that you can escape. Keep your eyes on the attacker as you assume an alert Defense Ready position. Watch for possible follow-up attacks from the original assailant or from his friends, and then get away to a safe place as quickly as you can.

LESSON 6 PART 3

Defense Against Double Wrist Grab Attack - Target Drill

Use a target pad drill version of the series to develop power, accuracy, timing, and balance in movement as you practice the techniques of the defense. A trainer wears large boxing gloves with articulated thumbs, and a firm target pad strapped to his chest to give you a safe striking surface you can hit with full power.

1. Start in a guarded confrontation preparation posture with your hands held up in warding off position, with a gap of just a bit further than one extended arm length between the center of your chest and the center of the attacker's chest.

2. Trainer reaches out and grabs your right wrist in his left hand and your left wrist in his right hand and pulls your wrists close to each other, wearing large boxing gloves with articulated thumbs so that his hands are protected as he grabs your upraised wrists.

3.1

3.2

4.1

4.2

4.3

3. Rotate your wrists to where you can see your palms and then slam your two wrists towards each other sharply two or three times to bang together the trainer's two pad-protected thumbs.

4. Pull back with your right leg, and slice the outer edges of your palms down with a scissor action to knock his hands off your wrists. Shout the command *Stop it!* each time you bang his thumbs together and when you shear his hands away.

5. Trainer turns to his left and stacks his boxing glove hands in front of you so you can practice a forward driving strike with the palm of your hand as you shout the command *Back off!*

6. Keep your eyes on the trainer as you assume Defense Ready.

7. Though not illustrated here, the trainer again reaches out and grabs your right wrist in his left hand and your left wrist in his right hand, and this time pulls your hands apart.

8. Sink as though trying to pull away, and then suddenly lurch forward with a forehead ram up into the padding on his chest. Be sure to align your head and neck carefully so that your ramming action comes from a straight spine alignment from your seat to your forehead

9. Trainer turns to his left and stacks his boxing glove hands in front of you so you can practice a rising shin kick and then a forward push with the bottom of your right foot as you shout the command *Back off!*

10. Keep your eyes on the trainer as you assume left-forward Defense Ready.

Chapter Nine

FRONT BODY HOLDS AND RESTRAINTS

I n the Shinden Fudo Ryu classical samurai *taijutsu* unarmed defense method I learned in Japan, the strike and grapple fighting technique was referred to as *da-ken tai-jutsu*. *Da-ken* 打拳 in Japanese is "striking fist." *Tai* 体 translates as "body." Jutsu 術 is of course "art" or science.

Shinden Fudo Ryu style *da-ken tai-jutsu* practice uses natural body movement to take the adversary off balance and interrupt his assault in a fight. Then strikes propelled by the body in motion injure and knock him down. Flowing movement is key, which is quite different from martial arts that rely on first locking the feet in stance and then punching.

In ancient feudal days in Japan, warriors often wore pieces of armor that rendered outside surfaces of the limbs and torso invulnerable to strikes. Trying to hurt such targets by hitting with the hands was almost pointless, so the fighters of the Shinden Fudo school developed a way of slamming in with full body momentum, unbalancing their adversaries, and battering them with strikes and joint locks against targets the armor could not protect.

Toshitsugu Takamatsu, the teacher of my teacher, was born in the 1800s and died in the early 1970s shortly before my arrival in Japan for study. He is said to have begun his martial arts study with Shinden Fudo Ryu practice as a 6-year-old in his grandfather's training hall. Practice sometimes took place outdoors in nature, with the students testing out their movement and leverage against trees and boulders.

In our contemporary world, effective grab and grapple counters are an important part of your protector skills. When defending another or yourself from attack, you may have to grab and secure a person's body trunk to keep him from moving or escaping, or to prevent him from being forced into a dangerous area. It is also possible that you may need to use an equally strong and leveraged full-body clinch to secure an inanimate object in order to rescue or protect someone; you may need to lift a person over an obstacle, move a crate or piece of furniture, or pull an animal or collapsing material off another person.

LESSON 7 PART 1

Waist-Grasp Tackle

As a trained defender, you will need to know how to step forward quickly and use a full body clinch to secure another person around the waist with leverage and strength. In To-Shin Do taijutsu unarmed defender training, we call this a **waist grasp tackle.** Your shoulder presses against their midsection and your arms wrap around from the front. You then force them out of balance and move them or push them down as they struggle to get back in control of their footing.

1. Start in an alert awareness posture with your hands in position low in front of you. The aggressor steps in front of you and threatens to hit, shove, or grab your friend with his right hand, leaving you in a position outside the aggressor's right arm.

2. Push the person's hands away to clear the path to their center and then crouch deeply on flexed knees and charge forward with your right foot to push your right shoulder into the midsection and throw both arms around the waist.

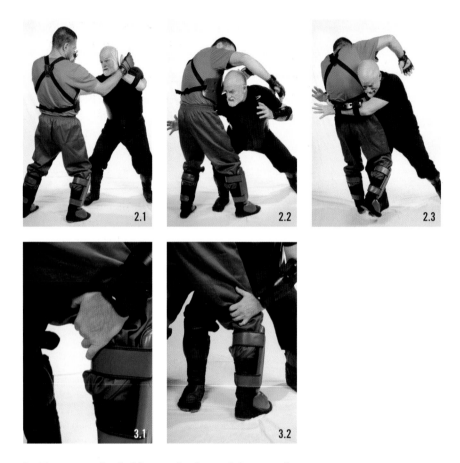

3. To secure the hold, you do three things at the *exact same moment*:

   • Step in deeply with your right foot

   • Lower your hips and push forward with your right shoulder to create leverage that will prevent him from pulling back from your advancing forward movement.

   • Tighten your arms to pull the aggressor's hips forward towards you
   as you push his upper body back and away from you with your
   shoulder. (Do not reach in and just hug them towards you.) If necessary for sufficient leverage to unbalance the person, you might
   reach for the backs of his knees and pull up and in as you push forward with your shoulder.

4. Once you have gripped the aggressor around the waist and moved him out of balance, keep moving forward and dump him down on the ground on his seat or back. Avoid just bending over in place and trying to wrestle the aggressor down with crude strength as he moves to regain his balance. Shout a growling command *Stop it!* as you take him down.

Try the same technique with your left foot forward and your left shoulder pushing into his midsection.

LESSON 7 PART 2

Defense Against a Waist-Grasp Tackle Attack

What if someone uses a strong and fast tackle as an aggressive attack to push you back or take you to the ground? If an aggressor charges in to grab you around the waist, you need to know how to defend right away and then disrupt and stop the assault and finally escape or reverse the grab to keep the aggressor from dominating you.

In To-Shin Do taijutsu unarmed defender training based on the Shinden Fudo Ryu practice exercises, we call this practice exercise *"Tai-hodoki"* **waist-grasp tackle defense**.

1. Start in a guarded confrontation preparation posture with your hands lifted in front of you in alert position, with a gap of just a bit further than one extended arm length between the center of your chest and the center of the attacker's chest.

2. Attacker knocks your hands away and then crouches and charges forward with his right foot to throw both arms around your waist or knees in order to lift you up or throw you down.

3. Sink to stabilize yourself on flexed knees, and jump back in coordination with his advancing forward movement. The key is to find and keep your stability as you move backwards to keep him from gaining leverage against your torso, being aware that he might try to reach for the backs of your knees.

4. Drive descending elbow strikes straight down to his back and head as you continue to step backwards, shouting the order *Stop it!*

5. Step back with your right leg and strike down on the back of his neck with your right hand-edge, keeping him away and off balance with left hand pressure on his right shoulder.

6. Swing your right knee up to strike him in the face one, two, or three times, shouting the growled *Stop it!* command with each knee to the head.

7. As the attacker collapses away from your kicks, lower your hips and shove him away with a loud command of *Back off!* Keep your eyes on

the attacker as you assume an alert left-forward Defense Ready position. Watch for possible follow-up attacks from the original assailant or from his friends, and then get away to a safe place as quickly as you can.

LESSON 7 PART 3

Waist-Grasp Tackle Escaping Defense - Target Drill

Use a target pad drill version of the series to develop power, accuracy, timing, and balance in movement as you practice the techniques of the escape. A trainer holds a large shield target pad by the handles on its sides to give you a safe striking surface you can hit with full power.

1. Start in a guarded confrontation preparation posture with your hands lifted in front of you in alert position, with a gap of just a bit further than one extended arm length between the center of your chest and the center of the attacker's chest.

2. Trainer holds a large shield target pad by the handles on its sides with the front striking surface aiming at the floor and the upper edge of the target aiming at your chest.

3. Trainer uses the target pad edge to knock aside your hands and then push forward at your stomach.

4. Jump back in coordination with his advancing forward movement, finding the back of the target as you move backwards.

5. Drive descending elbow strikes straight down to the target as you continue backwards, shouting the order *Stop it!*

6. Step back with your right leg and strike down on the target with your right hand-edge, keeping left hand pressure on the target.

7. Swing your right knee up to strike the bottom surface of the target one, two, or three times, shouting the growled *Stop it!* command with each knee impact.

8. Step backwards with your right foot and a possible follow-up kick to the target with your left foot, shouting the command *Back off!* Keep your eyes on the trainer as you assume left-forward Defense Ready.

LESSON 8 PART 1

Two-Hand Throat Grasp

As a trained defender, you will need to know how to step forward quickly and reach straight out to secure an attacker's neck with precision and strength in order to take con-trol of him and prevent him from doing harm. In To-Shin Do taijutsu unarmed defender training, we call this a ***two-hand grasp.*** Your two hands reach forward to grab a target in front of you, pushing a person back or guiding him to one side or another. As a rescue action, you might also use both hands to grab and lift a child to safety, or use both hands to grab an aggres-sor's arm as he hammers down with a weapon.

1. Start in a guarded confronta-tion preparation posture with your

hands low in front of you in alert position, with a gap of just a bit further than one extended arm length between the center of your chest and the center of the attacker's chest.

2. To secure the grab, you step forward with one foot and shoot your hands straight in to catch the aggressor's neck in both of your hands.

3. Push both palms in and down with firm pressure as you wrap your fingers around the back of his neck and press thumbs into the base of his throat.

4. Once you have gripped the aggressor's neck, push away as you step toward him. Shout a growling command *Stop it!*

5. Though not pictured here, you could turn to your left with flexing knees and wedge your right calf beside the aggressor's right lower leg to trip him and pull him sideways to the ground, away from the person you are rescuing. Step forward to pull the aggressor off balance. Avoid staying in place and trying to wrestle the aggressor down with crude jerking motions as he moves to regain his leverage.

A double-hand grip can be used to secure a dangerous moving limb.

1. An attacker might try to strike with a weapon while positioning you too far away to defend.

2. Crouch low beneath the attacker's point of leverage and leap in to grab his wrist as he pulls back to wind up for his strike.

3. Shift forward with your second gripping hand and further stabilize yourself as you immobilize the weapon arm and pull the aggressor off balance.

4. Use elbow or knee swing strikes to subdue the attacker. Avoid trying to wrestle the aggressor down with crude jerking motions as he moves to regain his balance.

LESSON 8 PART 2

Defense Against a Two-Hand Throat Choke Attack

What if someone uses their strong and precise two-handed grasp as an aggressive attack to choke your throat? If an aggressor reaches forward with both hands to grasp your neck, you need to know how to defend right away and then disrupt and stop the assault and finally escape or re-verse the grab to keep the aggressor from dominating you.

In To-Shin Do taijutsu unarmed defender training, we call this prac-tice exercise *"Ryo-te Gake"* **Escape from 2-hand throat choke**.

1. Start in a guarded confrontation preparation posture with your hands low in front of you in alert position, with a gap of just a bit further than

3.1

3.2

3.3

one extended arm length between the center of your chest and the center of the attacker's chest.

2. Attacker steps forward with his left foot and grabs your neck from the front with both of his hands. His grip holds you with his thumbs on the front of your windpipe and his fingers around the back of your neck.

3. Step back and lower your seat to stabilize yourself on flexed knees with your shoulders

4.1

4.2

4.5

over your hips, being aware that he might try to shove you into a wall or piece of furniture or to one side.

4. If the aggressor pulls you towards him or holds you in a position where your hands rise naturally along the outside of his forearms, swing both hands up high and then cut down with simultaneous hand-edge strikes to his wrists, then turn your fingers into downward pulling hooks. Keep your hands moving as you hit and pull down; do not grip and tug at his wrists. To reduce impact of driving his hands into your collarbones as you hit down, crouch on flexed knees and pull your torso backwards as you execute the movement, and shout a growling command *Stop it!* as you strike down with the edges of your hands.

5.1

5.2

5. As an alternate technique, if the aggressor pushes you backwards or holds you in a position where your hands rise naturally inside his forearms, lift your hands palm-to-palm between his wrists and swing both hands up high and back along the sides of your head. Lift your arms as

5.3

6

you hit and lift; do not merely bump upward with your wrists. Pull your torso backwards as you execute the movement, and shout a growling command *Stop it!* as you lift upward with your hands.

6. To continue from position inside the aggressor's wrists, regardless of using the inner or outer escape, pull your right shoulder back and rotate your left shoulder forward as you pierce with a left hand fingertip spear to the aggressor's eyes. A quick jab to the eyes will not do lasting damage, but will likely cause him to flinch back in surprise. Continue to shout the growled *Stop it!* command with each strike.

8.1

8.2

7. Follow with driving kicks to his thighs, hips, or lower abdomen, making impact with the bottom of your heel or the toe of your shoe. Continue to shout the command *Stop it!* with each strike.

8. It is possible that the attacker has such a strong grip, or that your timing fails to startle him, so that your lifting hands do not dislodge his grip. If that is the case, in another alternate technique, turn inward, reach over his forearms with your arm closest to him to knock both hands loose with your shoulder twist, and back-swing your elbow or hand-edge to his head, shouting the command *Stop it!* with your strike.

9. As the attacker collapses away from your strikes and kicks, lower your hips and back away with a loud command of *Back off!* Keep your eyes on the attacker as you assume an alert left-forward Defense Ready position. Watch for possible follow-up attacks from the original assailant or from his friends, and then get away to a safe place as quickly as you can.

LESSON 8 PART 3

Two-Hand Throat Choke Escaping Defense - Target Drill

Use a target pad drill version of the series to develop power, accuracy, timing, and balance in movement as you practice the techniques of the defense. A trainer wears boxing gloves or target pads on his forearms to give you a safe striking surface you can hit with full power.

1. Start in a guarded confrontation preparation posture with your hands low in front of you in alert position, with a gap of just a bit further than one extended arm length between the center of your chest and the center of the attacker's chest.

2. Wearing boxing gloves or pads on the tops of the forearm, trainer steps forward to press in on your collarbones with outstretched arms.

3. Lift your hands *outside* the training target pads and strike down as you crouch on flexed knees, hitting the trainer's pads with the edges of your hands, or...

4. Trainer wears striking pads on the inside of the forearms, or rotates boxing gloves to serve as protection and steps forward to press in on your collarbones.

5. Lift your hands *inside* the training target pads and swing your arms along the top and back of your head (or pop your hands outward against the trainer's wrists) as you crouch on flexed knees, hitting the trainer's pads as you lift your arms.

6. Trainer shifts to his right and turns to his left to a position with his right arm lifted with target stretched forward perpendicular to your path.

7. Rotate your left shoulder forward and tap the target with your left fingertips or drive in with the heel of your palm.

8. Additionally, the trainer can lower his right arm and support the target with his left.

9. Kick forward with your right leg, hitting the target with the toe of your right shoe.

10. Kick with your left leg, hitting the target with the bottom of your left heel. Shout the command *Stop it!* with each kick into the target.

11. Keep your eyes on the trainer as you back away in left-forward Defense Ready shouting the command *Back off!*

LESSON 9 PART 1

Single Lapel Grab

As a trained defender, you will need to know how to step forward quickly and reach straight out to secure and hold in place a potential attacker with pressure and leverage to lock him up and prevent his movement. In To-Shin Do taijutsu unarmed defender training, we call this a **single lapel grab.** Your hand grasps the coat or jacket lapel of the person in front of you.

1. Start in natural posture as the aggressor steps into position in front of you.

2. To secure the grab, you do three things at the *exact same moment:*

- Step forward with your right foot
- Push your right shoulder forward so your left shoulder pulls back—remember to keep your shoulders over your hips; do not lean your upper body forward

- Push the left side of the aggressor's chest with the palm of your right hand, and catch the fabric of his jacket with your curling fingers.

3. Push your right palm into his chest with firm pressure to facilitate a tight grasp. Press the right side of his chest with your upraised left palm to help unbalance him when he resists your grip. Shout a growling command *Stop it!* as you push him into an immoveable position.

4. If he tries to strike or grab with his free hand, hit down and out from inside his moving arm.

5. If he tries to kick, you can slam the bottom of your foot down for a jamming action to stop his leg.

Try the same technique with the aggressor moving with his right side forward. Reach out with a left grab to his right lapel.

LESSON 9 PART 2

Defense Against a Single Lapel Grab Attack

An aggressor could use a single lapel grab to intimidate and hold you in place, and this defensive rescue could then become an assault. If an aggressor reaches forward to grasp your jacket, you need to know how to defend right away and then disrupt and stop the assault and finally escape the grab to keep the aggressor from dominating you.

1   2   3.1

3.2

In To-Shin Do taijutsu unarmed defender training, we call this practice exercise *"Ho-soku"* **Forward facing single lapel grab defense**.

1. Start in a guarded confrontation preparation posture with your hands held low in alert position, with a gap of just a bit further than one extended arm length between the center of your chest and the center of the attacker's chest.

4.1   4.2

5.1   5.2   5.3

5.4

2. Attacker steps forward with his right foot and grabs your left lapel or jacket front with his right hand. He grabs the cloth and curls his right arm to where the elbow is low and the palm is facing upward in an up-close "in your face" intimidation grab holding you in place.

3. In a surprise motion, lift and drive your right knee sharply to his groin or thigh, shouting the order *Stop it!*

6.1   6.2

4. It is likely that the knee strike will cause his upper body to pitch forward, so lift your right forearm to shield your face, and then hammer down or over to the right side of his head with the bottom of your upraised right fist one, two, or three times.

5. Be sure you breathe powerfully to build and release your energy and prevent accidentally sucking your breath in. Shout a growling command *Stop it!* each time you hit his head or neck.

6. Step to your left and hit his right hand off your jacket with a right hand-edge strike to the inside of his right wrist, knocking him away with a loud command of *Back off!* In future advanced training, you will practice locking up and pinning down the aggressor to restrain him from

further attack, but for now just concentrate on getting free so that you can escape. Keep your eyes on the attacker as you assume an alert left-forward Defense Ready position. Watch for possible follow-up attacks from the original assailant or from his friends, and then get away to a safe place as quickly as you can.

LESSON 9 PART 3

Defense Against Single Lapel Grab Attack - Target Drill

Use a target pad drill version of the series to develop power, accuracy, timing, and balance in movement as you practice the techniques of the defense. A trainer wears a firm target pad on his left palm to give you a safe striking surface you can hit with full power.

1. Start in a guarded confrontation preparation posture with your hands held low in alert position, with a gap of just a bit further than one extended arm length

between the center of your chest and the center of the attacker's chest.

2. Trainer reaches out and touches your right lapel with his left hand and holds a target with striking surface aiming downward.

3. Quickly lift your left knee into the training target one or two times and shout the command *Stop it!* each time you hit upward with your knee.

4. Trainer lifts his right hand to his right shoulder with the training target striking surface aiming outward so you can practice one or two left body-twisting swinging hammer fist strikes as you shout the command *Stop it!*

5. Trainer steps back and away and lifts his left hand with the training target so you can practice a left hand-edge strike to the target as you shout the command *Back off!*

6. Keep your eyes on the trainer as you assume Defense Ready position.

Chapter Ten

CAPTURES AND RESTRAINTS FROM BEHIND

I n the classical ninja taijutsu unarmed defense methods I learned in Japan, piercing precision strikes were referred to as *kosshi-jutsu* 骨指 術. The *ko* 骨 of the Japanese word *kosshi* translates as "bone" or body frame. *Shi* 指 of *kosshi* translates as "finger," and less literally refers to the hands and feet at the ends of the arms and legs. In ninja taijutsu practice, the essence of *kosshi-jutsu* is your body weapons in motion to pierce and stun vulnerable points of the adversary's muscles, nerves, and organs.

In the Sengoku Jidai "Warring States era" of Japan five hundred years ago, Togakure Ryu ninja and Momochi family ninja of Iga practiced *kosshi-jutsu* of the Gyokko Ryu for training in the ability to strike with precision at key targets of an attacker's body and limbs. Gyokko Ryu kosshi-jutsu was in those days an exotic import from China, and legends told of the method being developed by a female guard of the ladies' quarters of a Chinese emperor.

Kosshi-jutsu taught circular footwork and precision striking unusual for Japan at that time, and featured strikes that drove the tips of the fingers and toes into targets of weakness. Photographs of Togakure Ryu master Toshitsugu Takamatsu in the 1950s show tough thick fingernails and toenails built up over years of intense training. My teacher told me that his teacher could tear bark off tree trunks with those formidable fingertips. Imagine what such weapons would do to a human neck or face.

Effective precision is still an important aspect of your defense abilities today. When protecting another or yourself from attack, you may have to grab and secure a person's body or limbs from behind to keep him from moving or escaping, or to take him away from a dangerous area. You may also need to use an equally strong and leveraged catch to secure an inanimate object in order to rescue or protect someone; you may need to lift a person over an obstacle, move a crate or piece of furniture, or pull an animal or collapsing material off another person.

LESSON 10 PART 1

Collar Grab from Behind

As a trained defender, you will need to know how to step forward quickly and use a clothing grab to secure or move another person from behind. In To-Shin Do taijutsu unarmed defender training, we call this a *collar grab from behind*.

You secure a grip on the back of their collar or jacket and wedge your forearm and elbow along their spine. You then force them out of balance and move them or pull them away as they struggle to get back in control of their footing. You could either use this technique to rescue a friend by grabbing his collar and moving him away from danger, or you could rescue a friend by grabbing from behind the collar of an aggressor as he moves forward against your friend.

1. Start in natural posture with your left foot forward and right foot in back. The aggressor stands in front of you with his back turned to you and threatens to hit, shove, or grab your friend.

2. Step forward with your right foot and grab with your right hand the collar at the back of the aggressor's neck.

3. To secure the hold, you do three things at the *exact same moment*:
   • Step in deeply with your right foot to be sure you have positional leverage once you grab
   • Lower your hips and push forward with your right shoulder to create enough pressure to permit you to secure a good grip on the cloth of his jacket or shirt
   • Flatten your forearm along his spine with your right hand holding his collar and your right elbow jammed into his lower back. (Do not reach in and just grab for cloth.) Push forward enough to create

instinctive resistance from him, which you will then capture and use to move him, but do not push so hard that you shove him forward into your friend.

4. Once you have gripped the aggressor by the collar and taken him off balance, pull back and down on his collar to cause his shoulders to fall backward as you push his hips forward with your right elbow at the base of his spine.

5.1

5.2

5. You can simply pull the aggressor back and trip him to the ground, or you can guide him to one side or the other with your footwork and body angling so that you can then lead him away. Avoid just bending over in place and trying to wrestle the aggressor down with crude strength as he moves to regain his balance. Shout a growling command *Stop it!* as you take him down.

You can also try a similar technique as a means of grabbing your friend from behind and pulling him away from an aggressor about to move against him.

LESSON 10 PART 2

Defense Against a Collar Grab from Behind Attack

What if someone uses a strong grab from behind as an aggressive attack to push or pull you off balance in order to take control of you? If an aggressor grabs your collar or jacket from behind, you need to know how to defend right away and then disrupt and stop the assault and finally escape or reverse the grab to keep the aggressor from dominating you.

In To-Shin Do taijutsu unarmed defender training based on the Gyokko Ryu practice exercises, we call this practice exercise *"Yubi-ku-daki"* **Rear collar grab**.

1. Start in a natural posture with your hands at your sides or lifted in front of you in alert position.

2. Attacker approaches from behind and grabs your collar at the base of your neck, pushing or pulling to force you off balance and into motion.

3. Sink to stabilize yourself on flexed knees, and turn to visually verify that this is an aggressor grabbing you, being mindful of possibly needing to protect against a strike from behind.

4. Pull forward with a big step and sideways turn, pulling forward in coordination with his shoving grab. The key is to find your stability as you move away from him. Straighten out his arm. Get your hips low and pull him off balance.

5. If you are grabbed with a right hand, swing your left arm upward with one, two, or three sharp quick back-knuckle strikes lifted to his ribs as you continue to pull away from him and straighten his arm. Be sure to avoid sideways swings to his ribs, as that will be too easy for him to jam with a palm-heel jam. Swing your arm up and in and get some momentum from a rocking motion on your crouched legs. Each time you hit him, shout the order *Stop it!*

6. Hit upward with your left palm under his right elbow and shove up with a blunt strike to dislodge his grabbing hand and knock his arm away. Slip backwards under his arm as it flies up and towards his front. As the attacker stumbles away from your hits, lower your hips and get behind him with a loud command of *Back off!* Later in more advanced training, you will practice capturing and taking charge of the aggressor to restrain him from further attack, but for now just concentrate on getting free so you can escape. Keep your eyes on the attacker as you assume an alert left-forward Defense Ready position. Watch for possible follow-up attacks from the original assailant or from his friends, and then get away to a safe place as quickly as you can.

LESSON 10 PART 3

Collar Grab from Behind Defense - Target Drill

Use a target pad drill version of the grab from behind to develop power, accuracy, timing, and balance in movement as you practice the techniques of the escape. A trainer holds a large shield target pad by the handles on its sides to give you a safe striking surface you can hit with full power.

1. Start with your back turned towards the trainer, with a gap of just a bit further than one extended arm length between your back and the center of the attacker's chest.

2. Trainer holds a large shield target pad by the handles on its sides with the front striking surface angling towards the floor and the upper edge of the target aiming at your upper back.

3. Trainer uses the target pad edge to push forward between your shoulders.

4. Step forward and turn to your side in coordination with his forward pressure as he follows you with the big target.

5.1

5.2

5. Swing your left arm upward with one, two, or three sharp quick back-knuckle strikes to the flat surface of the target as you continue to back away, shouting with each strike the order *Stop it!*

6. Following your hits, the trainer lifts and flattens the target so you have an imitation of the attacker's straightened elbow.

7. Hit upward with your left palm and knock the target away, shouting the command *Back off!*

7.2

LESSON 11 PART 1

Two-Hand Torso Grasp from Behind

As a trained defender, you will need to know how to step forward quickly and use a body grab to secure or move another person from behind. In To-Shin Do taijutsu unarmed defender training, we call this a *two-hand torso grasp from behind*.

You secure a grip on their shoulders or around their chest and then force them out of balance to move them or pull them away as they struggle to get free. You could use this technique to rescue your friend by grabbing him and moving him away from danger, or you could rescue a friend by grabbing from behind an aggressor as he moves forward against your friend.

1. Start in natural posture with your left foot forward and right foot in back. The aggressor stands in front of you with his back turned to you and threatens to hit, shove, or grab your friend.

2. Step forward with your right foot and grab with both hands the tops and sides of the aggressor's shoulders.

3. You could as well throw one shoulder forward and wrap both arms around his shoulders from behind, turning your head and pressing it against his back to keep from being bumped in the face.

4. To secure the hold, you do three things at the *exact same moment*:

   • Step in deeply with your right foot to be sure you have positional leverage once you grab; avoid having your feet in side-by-side stance where he could twist and throw you off balance

- Lower your hips and pull down on his shoulders to create enough pressure to permit you to secure a good grip on his frame
- Lower your elbows to add to your strength. (Do not reach in and just grab with your fingers.) Push forward enough to create instinctive resistance from him, which you will then capture and use to move him, but do not push so hard that you shove him forward into your friend.

5. Once you have gripped the aggressor by the shoulders or around the torso and taken him off balance, pull back and down and twist to the side to confuse his sense of balance.

6. You can simply pull the aggressor back and trip him to the ground, or you can guide him to one side or the other with your footwork and body angling to lead him away. Avoid just bending over in place and trying to wrestle the aggressor down with crude strength as he moves to regain his balance. Shout a growling command *Stop it!* as you move him.

You can also try a similar technique as a means of grabbing your friend from behind and pulling him away from danger.

LESSON 11 PART 2

Defense Against Two-Hand Torso Grasp from Behind

What if someone uses a strong grab from behind as an aggressive attack to force you off balance or restrain you? If an aggressor grabs your shoulders from behind, you need to know how to defend right away and then disrupt and stop the assault and finally escape the grab to keep the aggressor from dominating you.

In To-Shin Do taijutsu unarmed defender training, we call this practice exercise *"Ketsu-myaku"* **Rear shoulder grab (or choke) escape**.

1. Start in a natural posture with your hands at your sides or lifted in front of you in alert position.

2. Attacker approaches from behind and grabs your shoulders or upper arms from behind, pushing or pulling to force you into their control.

3. They could as well throw both arms around your upper arms to hold you down, or they could loop one arm around your neck and tighten it into a choke from behind.

4. Sink to stabilize yourself on flexed knees, and turn to visually verify that this is an aggressor grabbing you, being mindful of possibly needing to protect against a headbutt from behind.

5. Lean or pull to your left to pull your weight off your right foot and then throw one or two downward stomping kicks to the aggressor's foot arch, ankle, or shin, shouting the order *Stop it!*

6. Shoot your arm out in front of you and then drive your elbow back into his ribs or midsection one or two times. Reach forward as though punching an imaginary target in order to have sufficient strength and speed to hit him hard; you do not want to peck at him with little elbow taps. With each elbow hit, shout the command *Stop it!*

7. If he still persists, you can edge your torso sideways to him and rock backwards with the side of your crown to headbutt him in the face. Get low so that your head strikes come in from below.

8. As soon as his grip loosens, spin around to where you are facing him directly from the front. Keep your hips low to hold your balance, and throw short palm heel strikes at his chin or use both hands to shove and knock him backwards with the shouted order *Stop it!*

9. As the attacker stumbles away from your hits, lower your hips and pull away from him with a loud command of *Back off!* Later in more advanced training, you will practice capturing and taking charge of the aggressor to throw him to the ground or restrain him from further attack, but for now just concentrate on getting free so you can escape. Keep your eyes on the attacker as you assume an alert left-forward Defense Ready position. Watch for possible follow-up attacks from the original assailant or from his friends, and then get away to a safe place as quickly as you can.

7.4

8.1

8.2

9

LESSON 11 PART 3

Two-Hand Torso Grasp from Behind Defense - Target Drill

Use a target pad drill version of the grab from behind to develop power, accuracy, timing, and balance in movement as you practice the strikes leading to escape. A trainer holds a large shield target pad by the handles on its sides to give you a safe striking surface you can hit with full power.

1. Start with your back turned towards the trainer, with a gap of just a bit further than one extended arm length between your back and the center of the attacker's chest.

2. Trainer holds a large shield target pad with the front striking surface aiming at your back and steps forward and bumps the target against your shoulders. Crouch for stability and look over your shoulder to see who is there.

3. Lift your knee high and stamp down on the trainer's padded foot in-step.

4. Reach out in front and drive your elbow back into the target behind you one or two times, shouting the order, *Stop it!*

4.1

4.2

5.1

5.2

6.1

6.2

6.3

5. Crouch and use leg power to drive head butt strikes into the target.

6. Drive forward with palm heel hits into the striking surface of the target to move the trainer back and off balance, shouting the command *Back off!*

LESSON 12 PART 1

Arm Grasp from Behind

As a trained defender, you will need to know how to step in from behind and grab an arm to secure and hold in place or lead away a potential attacker. Your left hand grasps from below the right upper arm of the person in front of you. In To-Shin Do taijutsu unarmed defender training, we call this an ***arm grasp from behind***.

1. Start in natural posture and walk up from behind and beside an aggressor's right side as he approaches someone you need to protect.

2. Reach up and forward with your left hand and grab the aggressor's upper right arm with your fingers beneath the arm and your thumb along the outside of the arm—be sure to grasp the bone and muscle of the arm and not just pinch the fabric of his sleeve.

3. To secure the grab, you do three things at the *exact same moment*:

   • Step forward with your left foot

• Push your palm into the triceps of his arm and then tighten your grip—do not merely squeeze his arm and hope to hold him in place

• Shove his upper arm forward and up so your left hand lifts his right shoulder higher than the left, causing him to tilt to his left and lose his balance with more weight on his left foot than his right.

4. As you push your left palm into his right arm with firm pressure to facilitate a tight grasp, you then grip his right wrist with your right palm on top and your right thumb pointing towards his elbow.

5. Once you have gripped the aggressor's right wrist with your right hand, push his right arm up and forward as you step further forward with your left leg. Shout a growling command *Stop it!* as you push forward and lift his shoulder and arm.

6. Stay at just the right angle to keep him off balance as you walk forward with flexed knees to move him to where you want him.

Try the same technique with a right grab to the underside of the aggressor's left arm. Grab his left wrist with your left hand as you push up and away to move him forward.

LESSON 12 PART 2

Defense Against Arm Grasp from Behind Attack

An aggressor could use an arm grab from behind to make you go where you do not want to go or hold you in place, turning this defensive rescue into an assault. If an aggressor grabs your arm and takes control of your movement, you need to know how to defend right away and then disrupt and stop the assault and finally escape the grab to get to safety.

In To-Shin Do taijutsu unarmed defender training, we call this practice exercise *"Te-hodoki 2"* **Rear arm grasp escape**.

1. Start in a natural posture with your hands low at your sides, with the attacker behind you to your right.

2. Attacker steps forward with his left foot and grabs your right arm from beneath with his left hand, lifting and forcing you forward and off balance.

3. In a quick surprise motion, reach forward and then straight up and then behind you with a big circular rotation from the shoulder, lifting your straightened arm to pull your arm out of the aggressor's grasp. Reach out with your arm as far as you can and make the circle as big and fast as possible—avoid a tight little elbow lift. Surprise him with your shouted command *Stop it!*

4.2

5

4. Immediately lower your seat for balance and leverage and stamp down on his foot or scrape down his shin with a heel edge kick one or two times. Lift your knee high to get as much downward force as you can.

5. Be sure you breathe powerfully to build and release your energy and prevent accidentally sucking your breath in with the surprise. Shout a growling command *Stop it!* each time you stamp down with the kick.

6. Place your kicking foot behind his leg and twist into a rear hand

6.1

6.2

standing fist punch to his abdomen or ribs, knocking him back with a loud command of *Back off!* In future advanced training, you will practice following up with additional kicks and strikes to defeat the aggressor and dissuade him from further attack, but for now just concentrate on getting free and making your escape. Keep your eyes on the attacker as you assume an alert left-forward Defense Ready position. Watch for possible follow-up attacks from the original assailant or from his friends, and then get away to a safe place as quickly as you can.

LESSON 12 PART 3

Defense Against Arm Grasp from Behind - Target Drill

Use a target pad drill version of the series to develop power, accuracy, timing, and balance in movement as you practice the techniques of the defense. A trainer wears a firm target pad on his left palm and places a target pad on the floor near your right foot to give you safe striking surfaces you can hit with full power.

1. Start in a natural posture with your hands low at your sides, with the attacker behind you.

2. Attacker steps forward and shoves his left hand target beneath your arm.

3. When you feel the touch, reach up and around to pull your arm free. As you lift your arm, shout the command *Stop it!*

4. Lift your knee high and drive the bottom of your heel into the target. Stamp down with your foot on the target on the floor one or two times.

5. Trainer steps back and away and lifts his hand with the training target striking surface held level so you can practice a cross-body punch to the target as you shout the command *Back off!*

6. Keep your eyes on the trainer as you assume Defense Ready position.

5.1

5.2

5.3

Chapter Eleven

WHY THE NINJA APPROACH IS BETTER THAN THE SAMURAI

I n old Japan, the *samurai* warrior aristocrats held final authority for enforcing the territorial boundaries and laws that provided for safety and security in the community. The samurai's job was to be sure that everything in the community ran in a harmonious and productive manner. Ultimately, when all else had failed, it was their duty to use killing force to maintain the peace when all normal rational means had failed. As with their knight counterparts in medieval Europe, the feudal Japanese samurai was a soldier, law enforcer, detective, judge, and executioner all in one person. In today's America, there is nothing even remotely like the honorable samurai and their broad peace enforcing responsibilities.

Indeed, some people see our culture as being as far away from that samurai ideal as is possible to imagine. Some argue that the law has lost its power as a crime deterrent for many in our society. Perhaps you have read of cases in which the victim of a crime received more scorn than the criminal perpetrator. Maybe you have heard of cases in which a terrified innocent citizen was punished more severely than the callous attacker, under the justification that the victim went "too far" in the degree of defensive measures taken. Perhaps you have heard of cases where the victim was forced to wait for their murder, because authorities could do nothing until the stalking killer actually committed a crime. Where is the possibility for honorably taking responsibility for personal defense in a society that seems bent on legally blunting personal responsibility for security?

You are not a samurai. You do not have the legal right or duty to capture and then judge and punish a lawbreaker. If you are confronted by an aggressor who goes out of his way to invade your life, your options are not by any means clear cut. First you must choose the most feasible way to contend with his contempt for your dignity, decency, and life. You must also anticipate the wide range of potential legal and social reactions to your defense. Once you win, you may have to deal with a wide range of backlash responses. You could be fined or imprisoned on criminal charges for carrying a weapon or for having studied some form of martial art and then hurting the person who assaulted you. You could be charged for damages in a civil suit after you injure an invader or rapist in defense of yourself.

Twisting the law for the benefit of the criminal is bad enough, but your danger does not stop there. If you fight back and win against an assailant's attack, your original aggressor may wait and return to strike later for revenge, retribution, or the satisfaction of "evening the score," and there is little you can do legally to prevent the attack you know is coming.

Advantages of Invisible Accomplishment

In these oddly confusing days of the 21st Century, when the victim can be punished and the criminal shielded by the legal system, perhaps the approach of the ninja is the fitting choice. The way of winning without attracting attention or animosity or resentment seems most intelligent.

In this age of envy, the masses seem bent on punishing anyone who excels beyond commonly accepted levels of mediocrity. Be too good, or too free, or too happy, or too pretty, or too kind, and you attract the resentment of those beneath you. Perhaps the battle tactics of the ninja, like those of the folk tale Br'er Rabbit begging his dull-witted enemy Br'er Bear to do *anything* to him but throw him into that awful briar patch (where the rabbit lives!), are most shrewd. The strategies of feudal Japan's invisible warriors suggest a different way of enjoying victory for those of us who live in the culture of upside-down values in this current age.

In ancient Japan, the samurai government eventually turned into a suffocating burden. It was so efficient in maintaining order that it eventually became too effective in preventing growth. The powerful forces maintaining the status quo stamped out any possible expression of original thought or new approach to social or legal advancement. This drove the Japanese people into centuries of isolation that ended with the surprise of American gunboats pulling into Tokyo bay in the mid-1800s.

Such extreme control produced an illegal underground cultural counter-force in opposition to the absolute legal, political, and taxation authority of the samurai in control of society. Japan's famous (or infamous, depending on whose story you prefer) ninja phantom warriors were the harassing thorn in the side of those charged with the maintenance of undisputed law and order. Defying the protocols of conventional warfare, the vastly out-numbered and out-classed ninja waged war to protect their families and homelands in ways previously undreamed of by tradition-bound samurai. Prohibited by law from owning weapons and engaging in "honorable" warfare, the ninja instead relied on cunning strategies that employed methods of psychological warfare, unconventional tactics, and skill with a wide array of ingeniously improvised combat tools.

The ninja also developed an unconventional approach to the philosophy of war. In most cases, the ninja was inevitably inferior in supplies and troops to the warrior aristocrats charged with eliminating any opposition. Therefore, conventional definitions of victory would not work for the underground resistance families. A new way of winning had to be conceived. A method for getting what was needed without attracting the attention or wrath of enemies had to be developed. There had to be a way to protect against danger without attracting the ire of that danger.

This new way of victory without the appearance of victory is what gave the ninja their name. *Nin* of ninja means to persevere, to endure, or to put up with physical or emotional discomfort that would be intolerable to others. Also pronounced *shinobi*, the written letter character for *nin* of ninjutsu came to imply concealment, imperceptibility to the senses of others, and the confusing quality of leaving others unsure of what they had just seen or heard or thought following an encounter with the ninja.

The bold formal honor of the samurai dictated a proper way of doing things that took precedence over all else, including success itself. In a world of absolutes, living up to the ideal was what mattered. Even failure could be seen as a sort of success by the noble samurai, as long as the detailed steps of the ideal were followed with righteous commitment.

In contrast, the ninja adopted a radically different view of honor emphasizing results. The ninja of feudal Japan then came to be known as "invisible warriors" because of their ways of winning in a manner that confused the enemy or even left the enemy with the impression that the ninja had indeed been defeated and was no longer a problem needing attention.

A Popular Mistake of the Late 20th Century

In the late twentieth century, it became fashionable to speak of conducting business in a way that provided equally beneficial results for all participants. This enlightened approach to dealing with the ages-old dynamics of opposition came to be known in popular vernacular of the time as "creating a win-win situation." You win and get something you want, and I win and get something I want, too. We both win. The honorable win-win situation became a popularly voiced aspiration for many who had grown tired of the old adversarial dynamics previously expected in any contest of interests or clash of wills. The win-win ideal is the objective of any negotiation between persons of broad vision and character.

Unfortunately, you will not always find yourself in negotiation with enlightened persons. There are some truly vicious and abusive individuals out there who believe that the only way they can win is to clearly identify someone else as a loser. Win-win has no attraction whatsoever for those who are unsure of their boundaries. If there is any doubt as to what benefits could or should be theirs, the insecure will always suspect that *more* could have been due them. The thought of your winning, even though they may have gotten more than they asked for, is intolerable. Such persons have taught themselves to believe that the world will always victimize the weak. They are convinced that the only way to avoid becoming victimized is to force someone else into the position of weakness. These hyper-aggressive competitors will not accept win-win. They are only satisfied with "I win, so you must lose."

This mindset is perhaps not so base or negative as it might sound in this description. Even the most ardent of win-win promoters will experience occasional twinges of uncertainty. "I may have agreed too fast," can haunt the happiness of any perceived triumph. You conclude a negotiation, get the terms you fought for, and feel happy with the outcome. How do you then feel when across the room the oppositional party members are grinning, winking, and giving each other thumbs-up gestures? You decide to end a draining and constricting relationship with a long-time lover who has turned sour. How do you then feel when your lover beats you to the punch and announces that the affair is over because he or she has found an exciting new person better suited for a relationship?

When any struggle moves beyond the boundaries of the familiar or confidence inspiring, where we know just what winning looks like, win-win can seem like a cop-out excuse for weakness. You can end up secretly fearing that you could have gotten more. Your hopeful commitment to the noble you-win-I-win approach becomes as much an embarrassment as a yellow happy-face "we care" button on the lapel of an insolent store clerk.

Sometimes, the only way certain people will be happy with their good fortune is to be able to think that they successfully deprived *you* of any good fortune. If you do not have the time to indulge these twisted individuals, you will need a tactic to accommodate their skewed outlook on life without dragging you down or pulling you into a fight you do not care about winning. You will have to think like a ninja.

In some cases of confrontation or conflict, it may be best to pursue your goals while encouraging others to believe the illusion that they are the winners. You become the ninja. Win-win is replaced in the mind of your adversary with a more stimulating "I-*think*-I-won-and-you-lost." That is what many people really want to believe in order to consider themselves happy with an outcome. Look discouraged and offended that the lover you were about to dump has found someone else. Boy did you show me! Suck wind through your teeth and shake your head and mumble that the boss is going to blow up when he hears how much discount this clever customer here talked you into offering. Aren't you the lucky winner! Purse your lips, look away, and offer a begrudging handshake to congratulate the co-worker who connived to beat you out of the position you pretended to seek in order to prevent interference with your pursuit of the promotion you really wanted. You got me, you relentless campaigner!

The ninja's *kyo-jitsu ten-kan ho* "juxtaposition of truth and falsehood" is the strategy of promoting a false sense of understanding in the enemy's mind. This is far more sophisticated than mere lying or fraud. *Kyo-jitsu* is the encouragement of your adversaries to see things just as they *want to see them*. You allow your attackers to believe in what is dictated by conventional common sense. You permit them to fall victim to their own beliefs as limitations. You get what you want. They get what they need. Everybody ends up *thinking* they are happy, even those perverse people who do not know how to be happy as long as someone else is enjoying life.

This way of attaining victory later came to be known as the ninja's subtle "art of winning." Why not investigate further to discover your own ability to utilize this gentle and discrete method? With some new knowledge about how we as humans operate when under the pressure of conflict, you can better fit into the flow of potentially destructive energies at work around you. Unobserved and unseen in the shadows, you can develop the ancient Japanese warrior art of obtaining that which you need while making the world a better place because you have attained your goals.

The Tuttle Story: "Books to Span the East and West"

Most people are surprised to learn that the world's largest publisher of books on Asia had very humble beginnings in the tiny American state of Vermont. The company's founder, Charles Tuttle, came from a New England family steeped in publishing, and his first love was books—especially old and rare editions.

Tuttle's father was a noted antiquarian dealer in Rutland, Vermont. Young Charles honed his knowledge of the trade working in the family bookstore, and later in the rare books section of Columbia University Library. His passion for beautiful books—old and new—never wavered through his long career as a bookseller and publisher.

After graduating from Harvard, Tuttle enlisted in the military and in 1945 was sent to Tokyo to work on General Douglas MacArthur's staff. He was tasked with helping to revive the Japanese publishing industry, which had been utterly devastated by the war. After his tour of duty was completed, he left the military, married a talented and beautiful singer, Reiko Chiba, and in 1948 began several successful business ventures.

To his astonishment, Tuttle discovered that postwar Tokyo was actually a booklover's paradise. He befriended dealers in the Kanda district and began supplying rare Japanese editions to American libraries. He also imported American books to sell to the thousands of GIs stationed in Japan. By 1949, Tuttle's business was thriving, and he opened Tokyo's very first English-language bookstore in the Takashimaya Department Store in Ginza, to great success. Two years later, he began publishing books to fulfill the growing interest of foreigners in all things Asian.

Though a westerner, Tuttle was hugely instrumental in bringing a knowledge of Japan and Asia to a world hungry for information about the East. By the time of his death in 1993, he had published over 6,000 books on Asian culture, history and art—a legacy honored by Emperor Hirohito in 1983 with the "Order of the Sacred Treasure," the highest honor Japan bestows upon a non-Japanese.

The Tuttle company today maintains an active backlist of some 1,500 titles, many

of which have been continuously in print since the 1950s and 1960s—a great testament to Charles Tuttle's skill as a publisher. More than 60 years after its founding, Tuttle Publishing is more active today than at any time in its history, still inspired by Charles Tuttle's core mission—to publish fine books to span the East and West and provide a greater understanding of each.